Map by University of Nevada, Reno

with Tree Hunts!

A VISITOR'S GUIDE
TO THE

University of Nevada, Reno Arboretum

James W. Hulse · Cheryll Glotfelty
Rod Haulenbeek

UNIVERSITY OF NEVADA PRESS | *Reno & Las Vegas*

University of Nevada Press | Reno, Nevada 89557 USA
www.unpress.nevada.edu
Photos © Cheryll Glotfelty unless otherwise noted
Front cover photo credits: (*background*) Cheryll Glotfelty; (*bottom left*) Jean Dixon;
    (*bottom middle*) courtesy of the University Archives, University of Nevada,
    Reno Libraries; (*bottom right*) Matt Zytkoskee
Design by Daniel Putney

LIBRARY OF CONGRESS CATALOGING-IN-PUBLICATION DATA
Names: Hulse, James W., author. | Glotfelty, Cheryll, author. | Haulenbeek, Rod,
    author.
Title: A visitor's guide to the University of Nevada, Reno Arboretum /
    by James W. Hulse, Cheryll Glotfelty, Rod Haulenbeek.
Description: Reno, Nevada : University of Nevada Press, 2018.
Identifiers: LCCN 2017046462 (print) | ISBN 978-1-943859-32-0 (pbk. : alk. paper) |
    ISBN 978-1-943859-33-7 (e-book)
Subjects: LCSH: University of Nevada, Reno. | Arboretums—Nevada—Reno—
    Guidebooks.
Classification: LCC QK480.U62 N35 2018 (print) | DDC 582.16/073—dc23
LC record available at https://lccn.loc.gov/2017046462

The paper used in this book meets the requirements of American
National Standard for Information Sciences—Permanence of Paper
for Printed Library Materials, ANSI/NISO Z39.48-1992 (R2002).

FIRST PRINTING

Manufactured in the United States of America

Contents

✿

University of Nevada, Reno Arboretum Board Chairs

Ed Kleiner, 1969–

Richard Post

Ed Kleiner

Wayne Johnson, 1978–1981

Al Mundt, 1981–1983

Anne Amaral, 1983–1985

Terrill Kramer, 1985–1988

Ginny Kersey, 1988–1991

Dick Garrett, 1991–1992

Skip Records, 1992–1996

Harvey Lambert, 1996–1999

Richard Post, 1999–2002

Bill Mize, 2002–2008

Raymond Needham, 2008–2014

Cheryll Glotfelty, 2014–

A Visitor's Guide to the
University of Nevada, Reno Arboretum

Springtime cowboy. Photo by Jean Dixon.

Introduction

*Plant trees. They give us two of the most crucial
elements for our survival: oxygen and books.*

—A. WHITNEY BROWN

Imagine yourself taking a pleasant stroll through the campus of the University of Nevada, Reno. You pause now and then to admire the stately buildings and beautiful grounds, and you wonder about the history of this place. You might even ask yourself, "Where is the arboretum?"

Fortunately, at your side are three friendly guides. One is a gentle, emeritus history professor by the name of Jim Hulse. Jim is a fount of knowledge about the university and can tell you about the buildings and the growth of the campus since its origins in 1885. The second, Cheryll Glotfelty, is an outdoorsy English professor; she chairs the Arboretum

Summer fun. Photo by Matt Zytkoskee.

Fall on the Quad. Photo by Jean Dixon.

Winter fun. Photo courtesy of University of Nevada, Reno.

Board and can fill you in on its activities. The third guide is a hyperactive tree enthusiast named Rod Haulenbeek, who can help you identify the 250-plus tree species and varieties on campus and delight you with fun facts about them.

The next best thing to enjoying the company of Jim, Cheryll, and Rod is having their words at hand in this visitor's guide. These pages trace the coevolution of the university and its landscaping. You'll learn how the entire

University of Nevada, Reno campus became a Nevada State Arboretum in 1985 and thirty years later a Tree Campus USA.

Each chapter focuses on a walkable area of campus, keyed to the map on the first page of this book. Proceeding south to north, from the oldest to the newest parts of campus, the chapters capture the unique character of buildings, gardens, and groves.

 There is a fun "tree hunt" aspect to this guide in that we highlight three notable trees in each chapter. If you find all of the trees in this book, you will have learned about more than fifty different species. The clues to these trees' locations often refer to the points of the compass. An easy way to get oriented is to remember that the Sierra mountains are to the west and the city center of Reno is to the south of campus. If your left shoulder aims at the mountains and you have your back to Reno, you'll be facing north.

For the diehard tree enthusiast, Appendix A provides a list of the 250-plus tree species and cultivars on campus; Appendix B, a list of 42 state champion / co-champion / up-and-coming trees at the university; and Appendix C, a list of 120 memorial trees.

Whether you are a local resident or visitor from out of town, we hope that this guide will enhance your enjoyment of the University of Nevada, Reno, and introduce you to the many interesting trees that populate the arboretum.

Arboretum in a Goblet

Trees are poems that the earth writes upon the sky.

—KAHLIL GIBRAN, *SAND AND FOAM*

Viewed from above or on a map, the University of Nevada, Reno campus resembles a goblet, one of those traditional water glasses with a wide base, slanting inward to a narrow middle, then curving outward to a broad rim. The base is Ninth Street, which parallels the Orr Ditch; the rim is at North McCarran ring road.

Ten acres of this land at the bottom of the goblet became the home of Nevada State University in 1885 and the site of one of the state's original arboreta one hundred years later.

The university "goblet" from the air, looking north.
Photo courtesy of University of Nevada, Reno.

University of Nevada sign at the corner of Ninth Street
and N. Virginia Street. Trees: Juniper lower left, weeping
Atlas cedar lower right, European white elm upper right.

University students painting *en plein air* by
Orr Ditch, c. 1905. Photo courtesy of University
Archives, University of Nevada, Reno Libraries.

Red hot poker flower.
Photo by Matt Zytkoskee.

Orr Ditch, south of Sarah
Fleischmann Building.

This goblet holds, in its bottom section, Nevada's earliest effort to turn the desert into an academy within a garden setting. A stroll through the campus today foliates this idea.

The University of Nevada, Reno has been an evolving laboratory for more than a century, experimenting in landscaping as well as academics. The faculty has had an arboretum committee since 1969, sixteen years before the campus became a state arboretum in 1985.

Tree Hunt

 Go to the intersection of North Virginia Street and Ninth Street 1 and find the UNIVERSITY OF NEVADA, RENO concrete sign.

JUNIPER The bushy evergreen tree on the left side of the sign is juniper (*Juniperus sp.*). This is the second-most-planted genus of tree on campus after pine, with over three hundred trees; but species differentiation is difficult for junipers. The one thing junipers have in common is small blue-gray berries, whose favorite use is flavoring gin . . .

WEEPING ATLAS CEDAR The blue-gray weeping conifer on the right end of the UNIVERSITY OF NEVADA, RENO sign is a fine example of weeping Atlas cedar (*Cedrus atlantica* 'Glauca Pendula'). It is a cultivar of Atlas cedar, a tree native to the Atlas Mountains of Morocco and Algeria. This cultivar is prized for its limbs which head in one direction at a low angle and continue as the tree grows. If you plant one of these, be careful in which direction you plant it.

EUROPEAN WHITE ELM Walk on the sidewalk along Ninth Street toward the Center Street entrance to campus. The large trees in a line along the sidewalk to your left are European white elms (*Ulmus laevis*, probably planted around 1910), native to Europe. Once the inconspicuous green-to-red-violet flowers have appeared, toothed leaves with uneven bases emerge. The fourth tree from the Center Street entrance is the Nevada State Champion, the largest of its kind in the state.

2

Sagebrush Hill

*The best time to plant a tree is twenty
years ago. The second best time is now.*

—CHINESE PROVERB

W hen Nevada State University (NSU) moved to Reno from its original
home in Elko in 1885–1886, the Regents selected a few acres on a
hill about a mile north of the town center. Reno was less than twenty years
old, and the town had little greenery, except for the natural foliage along the
Truckee River.

Early university bulletins described the site as an "eminence." Its
location was a few feet higher than the valley floor, offering a panoramic
view of Mount Rose, Slide Mountain, and the Virginia Range.

Later generations called this place the "Hill" to distinguish it from the
"Town." When Morrill Hall with its three stories was completed in 1887, it

University campus, 1894. Morrill Hall is the third building from the left.
Photo courtesy of the Nevada Historical Society.

Morrill Hall, c. 2015. Photo courtesy of University of Nevada, Reno.

General view of campus, 1904. Scarcely a tree in sight.
The town of Reno sits in the background. Photo courtesy
of University Archives, University of Nevada, Reno Libraries.

Ninth Street hillside, south of Morrill Hall. Orr Ditch is out of sight at the top of the slope. The big tree trunk at right is an elm; the two big tree trunks to its left are eastern cottonwoods. Photo by Matt Zytkoskee.

University entrance gates, 1903. Photo courtesy of University Archives, University of Nevada, Reno Libraries.

looked down onto and beyond the trees of the community a mile away. But little green foliage existed up here yet. The few trees that were planted on the slope between Morrill Hall and Ninth Street are some of the oldest and tallest trees in the arboretum.

During the next twenty years, a dozen buildings appeared on the Hill—four of them in the Mansard style then popular in American colleges. The Hill remained mostly barren of trees and shrubs—except for the native sagebrush, rabbitbrush, and an occasional random planting—until President Joseph E. Stubbs became friends with Clarence Mackay, whose generous donations promoted campus greening.

Tree Hunt

Start on the sidewalk on the bridge where the Center Street entrance to campus crosses Orr Ditch **2**, one short block uphill from Ninth Street.

NORWAY SPRUCE The similar-looking evergreens in a group on the east side of Center Street, near the bridge, are Norway spruce (*Picea abies*, probably planted in the 1950s), native to central and northern Europe. Its branches tend to droop on each side of the limb, and the limbs tend to droop from the trunk. Its cones are 4 to 6 inches long and droop down from the limbs.

GREEN ASH The very tall tree growing on the grassy slope below and east of the Norway spruces is the Nevada State Champion green ash (*Fraxinus pennsylvanica*, probably planted about 1930), native to the eastern United States. This tree is desirable because of its bright-yellow color in early fall, but green ash trees all over Reno are susceptible to aphids (which curl up leaves but don't usually kill trees) and a new pest, the western ash borer, which has killed many mature green ashes in Reno.

EASTERN COTTONWOOD From the green ash, proceed northeast upslope about 25 yards toward Orr Ditch until you get to another towering tree. This is an eastern cottonwood (*Populus deltoides*, planted about 1905), which is native to the eastern half of North America. This tree is fast growing and provides both shade and windbreak to farms and towns in the Midwest. However, it has weak branches that constantly fall on lawns, as well as "cotton," the misty seeds that cause "snowstorms" in June. This tree's native habitat is along streams, so as a water sucker it is illegal to plant an eastern cottonwood in the City of Reno. The Nevada State Champion eastern cottonwood is the similar-looking, magnificent tree to the east (the second tree west of the stairway).

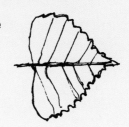

The Mackay Seedlings—Main Quad

Verde que te quiero verde.
Verde viento. Verdes ramas.
Green, how I want you green.
Green wind. Green branches.

—FEDERICO GARCÍA LORCA, "ROMANCE SONÁMBULO"

Landscaping ideas sprouted when Clarence Mackay made the first gifts to honor his father, John Mackay of Comstock Lode fame, who had been known for his legendary generosity. To perpetuate that heritage, Clarence made several gifts to Nevada U soon after 1908, in addition to the School of Mines and the statue of John Mackay by Gutzon Borglum, who also sculpted Mount Rushmore.

The bare, dirt field north of Morrill Hall was originally used as a parade ground for student cadets in the late 1800s. In 1907 Clarence Mackay financed the greening of the Quad, which was modeled after Thomas

Main Quad, 2015. Photo by Matt Zytkoskee.

Mules plowing the Quad, 1908. Photo courtesy of
University Archives, University of Nevada, Reno Libraries.

Jefferson's design of the University of
Virginia lawn.

The first landscapers chose elms
alternating with poplars—also known
as cottonwoods—to line the Mackay
Quadrangle, poplars being a species
favored by early pioneers. Planted on the
east and west sides of Mackay's Quad,
the poplars grew quickly and served for a
quarter century. In 1933 President Walter
E. Clark ordered that they be removed so
the slower-growing but longer-living elms
could thrive. The school yearbook that
year reported, "The university was turned
into a veritable lumber camp as the poplar
trees lining the quad were cut to make

Great Horned Owl roosting
in an elm tree on the Quad.
Photo by Jean Dixon.

room for the elms." In 1988, as the elms became vulnerable to Dutch elm
disease, a few of the original elms were removed, and they were joined by
other varieties.

Some elms have lost favor with many landscapers over the years,
but those now standing on the Quad have become iconic for sentimental
alumni. Campus planners have often heard suggestions that all thirty-six
should be replaced. During the long tenure of President Joe Crowley, when
a proposal reached his desk to remove them, his response was, "Not on
my watch!"

Scotch elm in front of Morrill Hall. This tree is the largest Scotch elm in Nevada. Photo by Jack Hursh.

Cane Rush, 1914, a popular game during this era, in which freshmen and sophomores battled for possession of a walking cane. Note the alternating poplar and elm trees. Here, the elms are dwarfed by poplars. The poplars were removed in 1933 to make room for the elms. Photo courtesy of University Archives, University of Nevada, Reno Libraries.

Disney on the Quad, one of the free summer concerts on the main Quad. Photo courtesy of University of Nevada, Reno.

As of 2017, a tentative consensus had been reached. A recent study implied the present community of elms can be sustained for several more decades. If there is a sacred grove on campus, this is it.

South of Morrill the botanical enhancements also invite reflection. For more than a half century, three majestic dawn redwoods (*Metasequoia*) and a Scotch elm (*Ulmus glabra*, labeled as the largest of its kind in Nevada) have earned tenure. They look down on Morrill, as if to remind us that their natural credentials are older than academia. The dawn redwood was long considered extinct, known only by the fossil record, until discovered in central China in the 1940s. Two European white birches (*Betula pendula*) share this part of the Hill with a cornucopia of springtime flowering companions.

Tree Hunt

 This tree hunt starts on the southeast corner of the main Quad near the Mackay Science Building ❸, wraps around Morrill Hall, and ends by the flagpole south of Morrill Hall.

ELM Around the perimeter of the Quad are thirty-six elms, a double row of twelve each flanking the walkway on the west side, and a single row on the east side. A historic *Tree Walk* brochure shows
the trees at the southeast and southwest corners of the Quad as European white elms (*Ulmus laevis*) and the trees next to them as Dutch elms (*Ulmus* x *hollandica*); a later brochure identifies Dutch elm and "hybrid elms." Elms are notoriously difficult to differentiate from one another, and the Quad sports a baffling mix of elm species. Whatever their scientific name, for many people the stately elm trees help make the Quad the centerpiece of campus.

JAPANESE PAGODA TREE On the south side of the Mackay Science Building is a tree with compound leaves. Now, what does that mean, exactly? Well, a compound leaf has a central petiole (leaf stalk) attached to the branch, with a number of leaflets coming out from it (in this case, twenty or thirty leaflets). A simple leaf may or may not be lobed, but it is never divided into separate leaflets. Most of the trees on campus have simple leaves. This tree is the Nevada State Co-Champion Japanese pagoda tree (*Sophora japonica*, recently renamed *Styphnolobium japonicum*, planted 1989). This native of China and Korea was introduced into non-Asian landscapes in 1747. Its compound leaves may cause it to be confused with black locust, but all confusion ceases in July or August when large clusters of yellow or white flowers appear. The seedpods, which look like strings of beads, stay on the tree all winter.

DAWN REDWOOD Make your way to the flagpole in front of Morrill Hall. Southwest of the flagpole you'll see a dawn redwood (*Metasequoia glyptostroboides*, probably planted around 1980) growing in the grass and another to the west of it. The branches of this tree arch upward, and the cones are egg-shaped with deep grooves that tend to go around the cone. This species was found in the wilds of China in 1947, and it has been imported all over the world. Its fast growth rate, interesting form, and russet-brown fall color before it loses its leaves make it a sought-after accent tree. Most conifers are evergreens, but the dawn redwood, bald cypress (featured in the Fleischmann Agriculture Quad tree hunt), and larch—deciduous conifers—are interesting exceptions.

4

Manzanita Lake and Bowl

For in the true nature of things, if we rightly consider, every green tree is far more glorious than if it were made of gold and silver.

—MARTIN LUTHER

Mackay's idea of a quadrangle, based on Thomas Jefferson's century-old model for the University of Virginia, was only one part of his plan for the greening of Nevada U.

The Hill slopes downward on the west and east sides of Morrill Hall as well as southward, and offered more options for landscaping as the young campus evolved. Mackay's 1908 plan included a sketch proposing a pond west of his quadrangle. This meant impounding water from the 1870s Orr irrigation ditch behind a dam, topped by a walkway commonly known as "the tram." It was the genesis of "the pond" (later renamed Manzanita Lake), on the upside, and the half bowl below.

Hot-air balloon over Manzanita Lake. Photo by Jean Dixon.

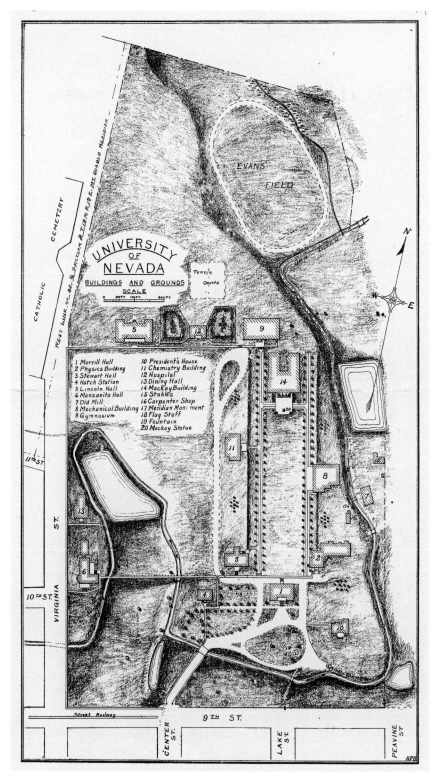

Nevada campus plans for growth, submitted to the
regents and the state legislature in 1908. Courtesy of
University Archives, University of Nevada, Reno Libraries.

"The tram" and Manzanita Hall, 1911. Photo courtesy of
University Archives, University of Nevada, Reno Libraries.

Lincoln Hall and Manzanita Pond, 1896. Photo courtesy of
University Archives, University of Nevada, Reno Libraries.

Winter sunset over Manzanita Lake. Photo by Jean Dixon.

Flowers and Manzanita Bowl. Photo by Matt Zytkoskee.

Along this sector of the south border (Ninth Street), are ten European white elms, and on the west (Virginia Street) is an arc of Hopa crabapples. Both species (or their near variants) were popular among early settlers in the Truckee Meadows, less favored by later generations.

The pond prompted several botanical experiments around its fringe. On the west side, next to Manzanita Hall, a rich assortment of flowering trees and shrubs thrives. Here Jimmie's Garden nourishes plants that

Jimmie's Garden. The orange-colored tree at left is a Japanese maple. To its right is a weeping Nootka cedar. Photo by Matt Zytkoskee.

prefer afternoon shade—including cherry, maple, magnolia, and several varieties of rhododendron and dogwood.

Between the pond and bowl stand two rows of Bradford pears, whose cheerful white petals celebrate the arrival of spring. As we circle around Manzanita Lake, flowering trees are interspersed with mature evergreens and deciduous varieties.

Before the mid-twentieth century, Lincoln Hall looked down upon the lake. A student in this dorm in the 1950s could glance up from his books for a brief Arcadian moment of reflection.

Tree Hunt

 The trees on this hunt grow in Jimmie's Garden, in the alcove on the east side of Manzanita Hall ❹.

PURPLE LEAF PLUM Go to Jimmie's Garden on the east side of Manzanita Hall. In the back-left corner of the alcove is a double-trunked, purple-leaved tree. This is purple leaf plum (*Prunus cerasifera* 'Krauter Vesuvius'). The species (cherry plum) is native to western Asia but has been planted in landscapes for at least four hundred years; this cultivar was named  for a nurseryman who introduced it in 1947, and it has become very popular because of its purple leaf color and contrasting flowers in early spring.

JAPANESE MAPLE The beautiful maple near the back-right corner of the alcove is Japanese maple (*Acer palmatum* 'Suminagashi'). Native to Japan, Korea, and China, Japanese maple hybridizes readily, and this is one of hundreds of cultivars available. Japanese maple is sought after because it stays relatively small, grows slowly, and has a controlled form (it is a major element of Japanese gardens). In Reno, it is best planted to the east or north of buildings to protect it from the prevailing winds.

WEEPING NOOTKA CEDAR The tall weeping tree at the end of the alcove— to the right of the Japanese maple—is a weeping Nootka (or Alaska) cedar (*Callitropsis nootkatensis* 'Pendula'). The species is native to mountainous areas along the US and Canadian west coasts. The sweeping, drooping branch structure is different on every tree, and this is an eye-catching evergreen tree.

5

Of Columns and Tree Trunks

*No town can fail of beauty, though its walks were
gutters and houses hovels, if venerable trees make
magnificent colonnades along its streets.*

—HENRY WARD BEECHER, *PROVERBS FROM PLYMOUTH PULPIT*

The three buildings that border Manzanita Lake on its east side—
Frandsen (1918), Thompson (1920), and Clark (1928)—became hosts
to another blend of trees: a northern red oak, a flowering crabapple, and
various maples and spruces, among others.

On the east fronts of Frandsen and Thompson, the Greek columns
previously introduced at Mackay Mines reappear, continuing the symmetry
inspired by the original Quad.

Thousands of years ago, in Minoan architecture, tree trunks were used
to support buildings. The stone columns fronting many of the buildings on
campus hearken back to their ancient roots as trees, harmonizing with the
university's arboretum.

Mackay Mines in the foreground, Thompson in the background, both
buildings fronted by columns. The pink flowering tree on the right is a
Blireana flowering plum. Photo courtesy of University of Nevada, Reno.

The David Hettich Garden in fall (*top left*).
Photo by Jean Dixon.

Virginia creeper vines in the fall, Frandsen
Humanities Building (*top right*). Photo by Jean Dixon.

A snowy first day of spring in front of Mackay Mines
(*right*). Reno weather . . . Photo by Jean Dixon.

The columns of the Mackay Science Building, which was added in 1930, and the Palmer Engineering Building, constructed in 1941, sustain the Ionic-Doric ideal introduced by Mackay.

Tree Hunt

 Stand in front of the main entrance (east side) of the Frandsen Humanities Building ⑤.

COLORADO BLUE SPRUCE If you stand on the plaza in front of the Frandsen Humanities Building, you'll see two very large Colorado blue spruces (*Picea pungens*, planted in 1917) guarding the building, one to the right and one to the left. Native to the northern Rocky Mountains, this tree sports beautiful blue-gray foliage, though it is susceptible to falling in winter storms and should be planted only in very sheltered locations. Older trees like these are not pyramidal in shape like younger ones. Red-tailed hawks and great horned owls frequently roost high up in these trees.

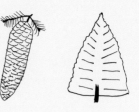

LONDON PLANETREE Between the Frandsen Humanities Building and the Thompson Building is a group of four large trees with light-colored, mottled, green-and-white bark. These are London planetrees (*Platanus* x *acerifolia*). This offspring of the American planetree and Oriental planetree was discovered in London in 1683. Since then it has been the dominant planetree, or sycamore, in both Europe and North America because it grows rapidly to a large size yet can be shaped, and because it is a resilient tree for cityscapes. It is identifiable by its maple-like leaves, its greenish-whitish, mottled bark, and its suspended fruit clusters made up of two beige balls.

BLACK OR EUROPEAN ALDER Now swivel around to look at Ross Hall to the east of the Frandsen and Thompson Buildings. The row of trees on the west side of Ross Hall, with numerous small dark "pine" cones and a darkish bark, are black or European alder (*Alnus glutinosa*), a European native popular when these trees were planted (probably in 1956, when this building was constructed). Black alder is an excellent pioneer species to plant in reclamation of degraded lands because it tolerates poor soils, grows quickly, and fixes atmospheric nitrogen that then becomes available to other plants. Black alder is uncommonly planted now, and has been supplanted by white alder (*Alnus rhombifolia*), a US native that has lighter-colored bark and not so many cones. The middle tree is the current Nevada State Champion.

Honor Court

A society grows great when old men plant trees
whose shade they know they shall never sit in.

—GREEK PROVERB

To the west of Morrill Hall is a relative newcomer to the older campus, the Honor Court, funded by private donations. Since 1997 it has been the home of a welcoming plaza for small ceremonies. It includes the Victorian gazebo and a thousand tons of polished, artfully assembled Sierra white granite. Here appear the names of donors and benefactors, along with faculty and students recognized for their achievements. During the last two decades, it has invited another cluster of trees and shrubs to enrich the botanical attractions of the Hill.

Moving down from the Hill into the Evans ravine, we find a subtle, new version of the proto-arboretum and the expansion of the university's mission. Here we descend into the watershed from Peavine Mountain.

Honor Court. Photo by Matt Zytkoskee.

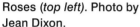

Roses (*top left*). Photo by Jean Dixon.

Wisteria growing on the honor-roll pillars of the Honor Court (*top right*). Photo by Jean Dixon.

Honor Court in fall (*right*). The yellow tree is a Princeton American elm, planted in honor of Bill Mize. Bill was the head of Grounds Services and Arboretum Board chair. The Princeton cultivar has shown great resistance to Dutch elm disease.

Its northward domain is the site of much of the campus expansion since the 1950s, expanding the resources of the arboretum.

The Hill is an experiment in high-desert hydrology, with two sources of water. Evans Creek comes down from Peavine Mountain, sometimes as a trickle, but occasionally as a flood. When the Sierra snowpack permits, the Orr Ditch flows from the Truckee in a more predictable manner. The botanical life of the Nevada campus adapts to these conditions.

Tree Hunt

The trees in this hunt are all visible from the Honor Court .

OHIO BUCKEYE Find the tall tree at the northwest corner of Morrill Hall. This is Ohio buckeye (*Aesculus glabra*). Native to the midwestern United States, this tree has hand-shaped leaves with five leaflets. In spring the tree has panicles, or loosely grouped clusters, of yellow-green flowers, which ripen to spiny fruits with brown nut-like seeds inside. Many parts of the tree are poisonous, but the Indians would roast, peel, and mash the nuts into a nutritious paste, the toxins being neutralized by the process. They also used the nuts to tan leather and to string necklaces. This tree has beautiful fall color.

NORTHERN CATALPA From the Ohio buckeye, head south toward the parking lot to the tall tree with the large heart-shaped leaves in the southeast corner of the Honor Court. This is a northern catalpa (*Catalpa speciosa*). Native to the midwestern United States, this tree has 6-inch-long panicles of white flowers in spring, followed in fall by dark brown pods about a foot long, giving it the nickname "cigar tree." Its wood is used for furniture and cabinetry because it has a beautiful grain and a low shrinkage/expansion rate.

SWEETGUM The young tree with maple-like leaves along the east-west walkway between the Rose Garden and Honor Court (just west of the Ohio buckeye) is sweetgum (*Liquidambar styraciflua*). Native to the eastern United States, its leaves have five smooth-edged lobes, and its fruit is spiny, 1-inch diameter balls. Note the ridges running along small branches of this tree. This is what is called "winged" or "corky" bark, and it is typical of young sweetgums. This tree, in the best color years, will have purplish, orange-red fall color.

7

Fleischmann Agriculture Quad

A fool sees not the same tree that a wise man sees.

—WILLIAM BLAKE, "THE MARRIAGE OF HEAVEN AND HELL"

T he ravine east of Morrill Hall invites us downhill into the Evans Creek watershed and another arboreal zone in the southeast corner of the goblet. This dip was not part of the original campus; it belonged to rancher John N. Evans (an early member of the Board of Regents), who leased this land to Nevada State U until about 1908 when Mackay bought it for the university.

Fleischmann Ag Quad. The big tree in the middle is a Scotch pine.
Photo by Matt Zytkoskee.

The Joe Robertson Garden, along the back wall of Fleischmann Ag Quad, features plants native to the Mojave and Great Basin deserts *(top left)*. Photo by Matt Zytkoskee.

Bald cypress is one of only a few deciduous conifers *(top right)*. The tree turns russet-colored every fall and drops its feather-like leaves.

Bee at work *(left)*. Photo by Jean Dixon.

A half century later, when the Max C. Fleischmann Foundation funded the Agriculture and Life Sciences Building in the mid-1950s, a second quadrangle (the Agriculture, or Ag, Quad) emerged, featuring a broader range of flora.

This square is host to the Joseph H. Robertson Garden, devoted mainly to flora native to Nevada. Robertson was a botanical scientist respected throughout the state and beyond. He introduced plants from the Mojave and Sonoran Deserts—a Joshua and yucca, among others—as well as northern Great Basin species. Elsewhere within this sector are trees suggesting the cosmopolitan nature of Robertson's interests—Canada red chokecherry, Port Orford cedar, Crimean linden, English oak, and the

The native plant Pollinator Garden. The white flower in front is tufted evening primrose; the purple flower in the background is Rocky Mountain penstemon; the orange flower in the background is desert globemallow; and the short purple flower behind the primrose is white pine skullcap.

ancient ginkgo. Robertson tended this garden for more than forty years—long after his retirement as professor.

Since 2015, in the narrow walkway leading north from the Ag Quad and around its perimeter, biologists have been experimenting with a wide variety of native flowering plants to attract butterflies and bees. This "Biggest Little Pollinator Garden" is being used to educate the public about ecology and the important role of pollinators.

Tree Hunt

Because the Fleischmann Ag Quad **7** is so botanically interesting, this hunt offers a special bonus of four trees.

BALD CYPRESS There are two tall bald cypress trees (*Taxodium distichum*, planted in the 1980s) growing near each other in the Fleischmann Ag Quad just east of the north-south sidewalk. The tallest of these is the Nevada State Champion. Native to the southeastern United States, bald cypress grows best in swamps (it is the star tree in swamp movies with its "knees"), but is tolerant of many sites. Bald cypress resembles dawn redwood (two are in the northeast corner of this quad), and you can compare them here: bald cypress has round cones with grooves that form polygons and has more or less horizontal branches; dawn redwood has egg-shaped cones with grooves that tend to go around the cone, and has upswept branches. Distinguishing between these two trees puts you ahead of the curve. Both of these unusual conifers are deciduous, turning brown in fall and dropping their feather-like leaves.

SCOTCH PINE The beautiful, large, full pine with reddish bark that stands alone in the southeast quadrant of the Fleischmann Ag Quad is Scotch pine (*Pinus sylvestris*, planted in the 1980s). It is very commonly planted locally and is often confused with Austrian pine, another European native. There are two major differences between these two trees. Notice that the Scotch pine's upper limbs are brown (the Austrian's are gray), and the upper limbs do not grow straight up like the Austrian's. This pine has bundles with two needles.

GINKGO Behind the Scotch pine is a concrete path with four square planter holes in a row. The trees with fan-shaped leaves that grow in these planters are ginkgos (*Ginkgo biloba*). The last tree in the row is the Nevada State Champion. Ginkgo is one of the oldest tree species still existing, first found in fossils around 150 million years old; it is now native to China, but was once found in North America. Trees are male or female; female trees are rarely planted anymore because the fruits are messy and have a disagreeable odor. The leaves turn bright yellow in the fall.

JOSHUA TREE In the Joseph H. Robertson Garden at the base of the Fleischmann Agriculture Building is the unmistakable Joshua tree (*Yucca brevifolia*, planted early 1960s), well adapted to aridity. A native of the Mojave Desert of southern Nevada and California, its leaves are bayonet-shaped, succulent, and have evolved to deter grazing animals. The Joshua tree grows only a few inches per year. This tree is a monocot—unlike almost all other trees at the university—and as such, it has no growth rings, so it is difficult to determine its age. Its white flowers, blooming in rare years, are in panicles (rounded bunches about 15 by 15 inches in size).

8

Engineering Quad

*A grove of giant redwoods or sequoias should be
kept just as we keep a great or beautiful cathedral.*

—THEODORE ROOSEVELT, *A BOOK-LOVER'S HOLIDAYS IN THE OPEN*

When tree walkers approach the Engineering Quad from the south,
they notice the Palmer Engineering Building with its Greek columns
(1941) on their right.

This part of the ravine was once shared by a greenhouse, tennis
courts, and (in the crowded years after WWII) several unsightly Quonset
huts that served for a few years as classrooms. When Scrugham
Engineering/Mines was built here in the 1960s, downhill from Mackay
Mines, another quad became available. Many of the trees that thrive here
today were planted in that transformative period.

Palmer Engineering (at right) and Scrugham Engineering/Mines (at left).
The red trees are red maple. The green tree to their left is northern red oak.
Photo by Jack Hursh.

Red horsechestnut in the fall. Photo by Jack Hursh.

Engineering Quad. An aspen is growing near the stairway at left. The two roundish trees on the lawn are red horsechestnuts, and the three tall conifers in the center back are giant sequoias. The bushy tree on the far left, growing close to the building, is red mulberry.

This plaza offers another venue for experiment and a botanical buffet for the eyes of meandering visitors. The beautiful red horse-chestnut that creates welcome summer shade in this verdant quad is a Nevada State Champion tree, the largest of its species in the state. Several giant sequoias found a home in this plaza sixty years ago. Most are still here.

On the western edge, tree walkers descending the stairs from the Mackay Quad are welcomed by a deodar cedar on the left and, on the right, locust trees, a Colorado blue spruce, and a Jeffrey pine. Near

Dog enjoying the Wolf Flow (*top*).
Photo by Matt Zytkoskee.

Daisy hybrids attracting a bee,
columbines behind (*left*).
Photo by Matt Zytkoskee.

A medley of spring flowers brightens
the Wolf Flow (*right*). Three young
aspens in the foreground; one big,
dark, deodar cedar behind.

the bottom of the long stairway, an apple and two Japanese maples offer
more greetings. Trickling under the stairs is a bubbling brook known as the
Wolf Flow in honor of Nevada's Wolf Pack sports. Here, in summer, you
can find columbine, blue flax, Shasta daisies, and other flowers blooming
in profusion under a cluster of young aspens, creating a miniriparian refuge
enjoyed by people, pets, and pollinators.

The very tall columns on the east side of the Paul Laxalt Mineral
Engineering Building (1987), just south of the Engineering Quad,
complement the much older Greek columns on the front of Palmer
Engineering. The Laxalt columns are much taller, of course, and lack the
Hellenic capitals, but they testify to the evolution of campus architecture as
well as the curriculum.

Tree Hunt

The trees on this hunt are all to be found in the Engineering Quad ⑧.
Have fun, and check out the sculpture at the base of the stairs, which
displays different types of structural steel supports.

RED HORSE-CHESTNUT The large rounded tree with two
trunks on the lawn to the left of the walkway to the Scrugham
Engineering/Mines Building is red horse-chestnut (*Aesculus* x
carnea 'Briotti,' planted 1963), a hybrid of two horse-chestnut
species. It is a very popular tree in England, with its 6-inch by
4-inch flower clusters reminiscent of common horse-chestnut.
Unlike common horse-chestnut, which has white flowers, red
horse-chestnut has flowers that are bright pink to pinkish red.
There are three of these trees in this quad; this one is the
Nevada State Champion.

RED MULBERRY Crowded against the south
face of the Scrugham Engineering/Mines
Building, to the left of the glass doors, is red
mulberry (*Morus rubra*), native to the eastern
and central United States. The leaves of this tree have one, two, or three lobes.
There are both male and female trees. This tree is probably a female. The tree
was planted too close to the building, offering a good lesson to homeowners:
when planting, bear in mind the tree's mature size.

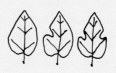

GIANT SEQUOIA The two enormous conical trees in the
northwest corner of the Engineering Quad are giant sequoia
(*Sequoiadendron giganteum*); many are present on the campus.
This native of the western slope of the Sierra Nevada grows
quickly and has a conical shape and awl-shaped needles. For a
tree that can grow to over 300 feet, it has astonishingly small
cones—just egg-sized. These trees are pretty big for having been
planted in 1963. This tree's preferred habitat is an elevation belt
where there is a lot of moisture (in the form of snow). It grows
quickly and can easily reach 100 feet in height within sixty or seventy years.
This tree has red-brown, spongy bark. Giant sequoias' thick bark helps them
resist fire, and high tannin content makes them insect-resistant; these are two
of the reasons that giant sequoias may live for over 3,500 years. If you look up
high in one of the trees, you may spot Tibetan prayer flags.

9

The Original Mackay Stadium and Hilliard Plaza

*Then the qualities, almost emotional, palpably
artistic, heroic, of a tree; so innocent and
harmless, yet so savage. It is, yet says nothing.*

—WALT WHITMAN, *SPECIMEN DAYS*

The next open space to the north was once Mackay Stadium. Here we had another echo from classical Greece—the oval suggesting the ancient Olympic games.

This sector of the Evans ravine, which was Mackay Stadium from 1908 until 1965, spawned another phase of arboretum pioneering. When the football field was relocated northward, more botanical innovations took root.

While this part of the ravine was still devoted to football, bleachers occupied the west slope. After the stadium moved north, the western slope was endowed with cedars of Lebanon, green ash, and mugo pines, which disappeared in the course of later construction. In 2017, a grove of two dozen ponderosa pines on this slope was cut down to make way for the University Arts Building.

Georgianna
Trexler Garden
in the foreground,
with Hilliard
Plaza behind.

Hilliard Plaza. The tall, blue-gray tree next to Mack Social Science (at left) is blue Atlas cedar. The row of dark trees against the Chemistry Building (front right) are columnar English oaks. The grove of ponderosa pines at far left has since been removed to make way for the University Arts Building.
Photo by Theresa Danna-Douglas.

1923 aerial view of campus. Morrill Hall is in center front. Old Mackay Stadium (at the top of the picture) was subsequently relocated to north campus and replaced by Hilliard Plaza. Photo courtesy of University Archives, University of Nevada, Reno Libraries.

Colorful fall foliage of a newly planted sassafras tree in Hilliard Plaza.

Blue Atlas cedar.

Three isolated London planetrees were once planted in the concrete planter beds sandwiched between the heating plant and Ansari Business Building. This trinity of sycamore relatives is a sanctuary for birds; cedar waxwings take nourishment among their branches, and boisterous chirping sometimes drowns out the industrial buzz of the heating plant.

In the center of the former stadium is the Albert Hilliard Plaza, named after a Reno attorney who served on the Board of Regents. In this sector a magnificent blue Atlas cedar presides. This lofty Nevada State Champion tree looks down upon an assortment of companions—a variety of evergreens and ornamentals that have given this place the label "Fall Foliage Area." We find here such varieties as the Kousa dogwood, black tupelo, silver maple, golden raintree, sassafras, European beech, honey locust, Young's weeping birch, weeping crabapple, and weeping sequoia.

Tree Hunt

For this hunt, make your way to Hilliard Plaza ❾, which is located between the Ansari Business Building and the Reynolds School of Journalism. There are some great trees in Hilliard Plaza, so we couldn't resist including a bonus fourth tree.

BLUE ATLAS CEDAR You'll have no problem spotting the largest tree in this quad, the blue Atlas cedar (*Cedrus atlantica* 'Glauca'), planted about 1970, on the west side of the quad, next to the Mack Social Science Building. The blue Atlas cedar is one of three "true cedars" that grow in Reno; all three are represented on the university campus. Blue Atlas cedar is native to the Atlas Mountains of Algeria and Morocco. Its upward-pointing white-to-beige cones can grow anywhere on the tree in winter. This tree can be identified by its pointed branches, and this particular tree is the Nevada State Champion.

YOUNG'S WEEPING BIRCH The broad, flat-headed tree near the center of Hilliard Plaza is a Young's weeping birch (*Betula pendula* 'Youngii'). This cultivar of European white birch (a native of Europe) was first introduced in 1873. It has a contorted branch structure and typical birch leaves with yellow fall color. Within this tree's drip line is an excellent place to wait out hot summer days.

COLUMNAR ENGLISH OAK Find the Chemistry Building at the southeast corner of Hilliard Plaza. Along this building's west-facing brick wall is a line of columnar English oaks (*Quercus robur* 'Fastigiata,' planted 1989). This is a cultivar of English oak, which is native to Europe, North Africa, and western Asia. Looking at this row of columnar English oaks shows just how much the shape of a particular cultivar can vary.

WEEPING GIANT SEQUOIA You have probably noticed the oddly shaped, sculptural-looking trees in various planter islands in Hilliard Plaza. This shapely humanoid tree is weeping giant sequoia (*Sequoiadendron giganteum* 'Pendula'), a cultivar of the sequoia species native to the west slope of the Sierra Nevada. Weeping giant sequoia has a vertical central trunk with branches that hang sharply down, nearly concealing the trunk; these trees are commonly used next to buildings. In some cases there are one or more "arms" angling out in different directions. Each "armed" tree has a different shape.

10

Pennington Center

What did the tree learn from the
earth to be able to talk with the sky?

—PABLO NERUDA, *THE BOOK OF QUESTIONS*

L ate in 2015 at the north end of the lower campus, near the narrowest part of the goblet, the Pennington Student Achievement Center emerged from the apparent chaos of construction. The landscaping plans around the Pennington behemoth became visible as 2015 ended. Some roses were saved from the Merriam A. Brown Rose Garden that once decorated the now demolished Getchell Library and were transplanted to a planter bed on the west side of the new building. Several older trees seem to have survived the stress of construction. One of them on the east side is a giant with a plaque certifying its status as the largest Dutch elm in Nevada.

Amur maple and samaras (seeds) in the foreground,
Pennington Student Achievement Center in the background.

This tall pin oak, behind the statue of Senator Richard Bryan, managed to survive construction of the new Pennington Student Achievement Center.

In other corners of campus, there are little islands of soil where nature lovers planted saplings near buildings fifty-plus years ago. In time they became the botanical counterparts of caged animals in a zoo. A majestic giant sequoia is imprisoned in a tiny space near the northeast corner of the old Virginia Street Gym, proud and defiant in its cramped circumstance. If this tree could think and feel, in the way that author Mary Austin of Owens Valley allowed her white-barked pine to do in *The Basket Woman*, it would likely ask, "What am I doing here?"

A monkey puzzle tree experiencing its first Reno winter.

For several months it seemed that the lower and upper parts of the campus were estranged, but the reconciliation became evident in 2016. The Pennington Student Achievement Center opened its doors and windows in the spring of that year, 130 years after the University of Nevada was transplanted from Elko to Reno. It seems likely to

A cramped giant sequoia tree. The Pennington Student Achievement Center is being built at rear left, 2015. Photo by Matt Zytkoskee.

become the focal point of both student life and new experiments with the cultivation of trees.

Located just south of the narrowest part of the goblet, the Pennington Student Achievement Center offers views both south to the lower campus, and north to the urban university changes of contemporary times. An elevator ride to the fourth floor offers testimony to this notion.

Looking southward, toward the lower campus, the tree lines tower above the older quadrangular buildings, and the Sierra ridgeline is much the same as the one the architects of Morrill Hall enjoyed in the 1880s. The treetops look down on the buildings, casting their morning and evening shadows on them.

Those who designed Pennington took care to create a spacious green swath at the south that blends with the lower, traditional campus. Several older trees were protected during construction, and young ones have been introduced.

The completed Pennington Student Achievement Center in the background (at left); construction for the University Arts Building in the foreground, 2017. Gone are the ponderosa pines that once grew on the slope to the left of the orange crane.

Rose.

When we look north from Pennington, we see the much-younger upper campus, with its multifaceted buildings and fewer trees. Around Pennington and farther north, we find many new plantings, experimenting like students with their new surroundings.

Tree Hunt

 For this tree hunt you'll walk around the outside of the Pennington Student Achievement Center, starting at the lower-level, sliding-glass doors on the north (back) side of the building **10**.

MONKEY PUZZLE TREE From the sunken plaza on the north side of the Pennington Student Achievement Center, look up at the elevated concrete planters adjacent to the outdoor flight of stairs. There are two unusual trees in this planter bed, alternating with the more familiar maple trees. These exotic evergreens are monkey puzzle trees (*Araucaria araucana*), native to the volcanic mountains of Chile and Argentina. This tree has dark-green, sharp, triangular leaves on its trunk and branches. Planted here on Arbor Day 2016, it was located at this site for two reasons: it needs some protection from our westerly winds, and the dagger-cloaked tree and the students need to be protected from each other!

LITTLELEAF LINDEN Now make your way along the east side of the building, heading toward the front of Pennington. Lining the sidewalk are young littleleaf lindens (*Tilia cordata*), native to Europe but planted all over since ancient times. This is a medium-sized tree with smaller leaves than its close relative American linden, but it has a nice shape. It has insignificant, but very fragrant, yellow flowers, and its seeds are generally not messy, so it is useful as a street tree.

PIN OAK From the statue of Richard Bryan in front of the Pennington Student Achievement Center, look toward the Ansari Business Building at the tall, somewhat spindly tree at the top of the hill on the lawn southwest of Ansari. This tree, a pin oak (*Quercus palustris*, planted 1982), managed to survive the removal of Getchell Library. It suffered some damage at the base of its trunk (note the painted wound), but appears to be doing fairly well. The lower branches of pin oaks tend to angle downward, while the upper branches extend out horizontally or trend upward, branch angle being a good way to identify pin oaks from other oaks. Pin oak, a native of the eastern United States, has deeply indented lobes and really nice yellow, red, russet, and/ or orange fall color, but some trees do poorly in Reno's alkaline soil.

In and Around the Raggio Building

Acts of creation are ordinarily reserved for gods and poets,
but humbler folk may circumvent this restriction if they know how.
To plant a pine, for example, one need . . . only own a good shovel.

—ALDO LEOPOLD, *A SAND COUNTY ALMANAC*

When the William J. Raggio Building arose in the late 1990s, the evolving arboretum met another challenge. On this slope, most of the trees are wrapped around the structure, rather than standing in an internal quad.

In the Raggio atrium, looking out.

Kwanzan cherries in bloom.

Outside, on the west, a row of Kwanzan cherries stands at attention. Almost all nursery ornamental plants, including flowering cherries, are grafted onto a related species with hardier roots. These Kwanzan trees are grafted at about five feet so that they will spread rather than grow taller.

Since the Raggio Building stands on a slope northeast of the Evans ravine, its outer circumference encouraged more arboreal experiments. It offers the opposite of a quadrangle; the most striking botanical innovations are inside. Here we are in a terrarium—four stories high.

Palm and ficus in the Raggio atrium.

Ponderosa pines south of the Raggio Building. Smoke tree (pink) and rabbitbrush (light gray).

Entering the Raggio Building from the doors on the east side, opposite Cain Hall, one is transported from the arid, high desert to the humid tropics in a single step. In the tropical microclimate of Raggio's atrium thrives a jungle of trees and shrubs that would never survive a Nevada winter. Here one may meet an enormous ficus tree, a Norfolk Island pine, and a yucca cane plant. A fiddle-leaf fig tree also grows in this verdant refuge, where it's summer the year round.

Tree Hunt

On this hunt you'll meet some ornamental cherry trees and learn to tell the difference between the imported but very common Austrian pine and the ponderosa pine. The trees on this hunt are found on the west side of the Raggio Building ⑪.

KWANZAN CHERRY The trees with reddish, smooth bark lining the front (west side) of the Raggio Building are Kwanzan cherries (*Prunus serrulata* 'Kwanzan,' planted 1999), one of the most popular of the Japanese flowering cherry hybrids. It has double pink flowers about 2 ½ inches in diameter that are hard to surpass in beauty. This tree is grafted at about 5 feet, and the branches above typically spread out.

AUSTRIAN PINE Exit the front doors on the west side of the Raggio Building. Where the walkway from Raggio intersects the heavily used north-south sidewalk from Hilliard Plaza to the Knowledge Center, note the cluster of medium-sized conifers with gray bark. These are Austrian pines (*Pinus nigra*), native to southern Europe. They are the most commonly planted tree species in this area, because they grow quickly to medium size and are resistant to pests. They have two needles in a bundle and 2-inch cones.

PONDEROSA PINE From the Austrian pines in front of the Raggio Building, turn left onto the sidewalk toward Hilliard Plaza. You'll see a grove of pines on the steep dirt slope to your left (below the southwest corner of Raggio). This tall conifer with 4-inch cones is ponderosa pine (*Pinus ponderosa*). It is native to the Sierra Nevada, mostly on the western side because its elevation range is 1,000 feet to 5,000 feet, and the tree line on the eastern side starts at 6,000 feet. This tree has three needles in a bundle, like its close relative the Jeffrey pine. Ponderosa pines are probably the most abundant tree species in the western United States. They have brown trunks, grow quickly, and can exceed 200 feet in height.

The Automobile Era and North Campus

A woodland in full color is awesome as a forest
fire, in magnitude at least, but a single tree is like
a dancing tongue of flame to warm the heart.

—HAL BORLAND, *SUNDIAL OF THE SEASONS*

The southern third of the campus evolved before the 1940s, when automobiles were incidental to campus life. Parking may have been an occasional problem for the few faculty and students who brought cars to the campus, but trees and shrubs still reigned here. Hollywood moviemakers chose the Hill for light comedies set in a bucolic college

The newer, north campus buildings, 2017. Joe Crowley Student Union at left, Mathewson-IGT Knowledge Center in the middle, E. L. Wiegand Fitness Center at far right. Note the relative sparsity and small size of the trees. Photo courtesy of University of Nevada, Reno.

NOTE: "12a" on the main map corresponds to the text of this chapter, while "12b" locates the tree hunt at the School of Medicine on the northern fringe of campus.

Arboretum Board and student volunteers planting a Japanese larch at the Medical School to diversify species and beautify north campus.

Each Arbor Day for the last dozen years, Raymond Needham (center), former Chair of the university Arboretum Board, plants one paw paw tree in front of the West Stadium Parking Complex. He is assisted here by Christoph Weber.

setting—*Mr. Belvedere Goes to College*, *Andy Hardy's Blonde Trouble*, *Margie*, *An Apartment for Peggy*, *Mother is a Freshman*, *Captive City*, *5 Against the House*, and *Hilda Crane*.

Gradually, during the past sixty years, the University of Nevada, Reno has grown tremendously, becoming an urban university, partner and successor to the original Nevada State University on the Hill. Most students, faculty, and staff drive to campus, and parking became and continues to be a pressing issue, illustrated by an anecdote from the Joe Crowley years.

When Joe was president (1978–2001), he offered an occasional "pizza break" to everyone—students, faculty, staff. Come to the student union, he said, for a free pizza. The only rule is, if you have a slice, you must ask a question or make a comment about life at the university. The bait worked, but half the remarks were, "What are you going to do about parking?" Joe often quipped, "This place needs two presidents. One for parking and one for everything else."

North of the goblet's narrow middle, where the vessel widens, the original sagebrush has been replaced by the Mathewson-IGT Knowledge Center, Joe Crowley Student Union, Wiegand Fitness Center, Lawlor Events

Sculpture of Leonardo da Vinci in front of Brian Whalen Parking Complex. The trees are summit ash.

Center, the second Mackay Stadium, the School of Medicine, and the necessary parking lots and garages.

On the upper campus, the arboretum is more timid and tentative than in the southern half. Most of the deciduous trees are younger, planted only a few years ago and more widely spaced among the pavers and concrete. Trees and shrubs, where they exist, are tucked into corners and slopes.

The arboretum also seems less interesting on the east side of the campus, confined by the railroad and Evans Avenue. Here are many of the essential maintenance buildings. The arboretum is sparser here, but many of the small older homes with their greenery compensate for the scarcity of campus trees.

Tree Hunt

 Be adventurous and trek up to the north end of campus for this tree hunt, which begins in front of the Savitt Medical Sciences Building **12b**, across the street from the Student Health Center. After you've located the three featured trees, explore the most hidden nooks of the arboretum—two outdoor courtyards, which must be accessed from *inside* the Savitt Medical Sciences Building and the Howard Medical Sciences Building.

TUPELO Face the double glass doors on the south side of the Savitt Medical Sciences Building. Turn left down the ramp next to the building and walk to the end of the ramp. Look at the westernmost tree in the grassy area to your left. This is tupelo (*Nyssa sylvatica*, planted 1987). It has smooth-edged leaves about the same size as a crabapple's, but its flowers are indistinct. Native to the southeastern United States, this slow-growing tree in the fall has brilliant red leaves interspersed with green leaves and yellow leaves, creating a parti-color splendor.

PAUL'S SCARLET HAWTHORN To the east of the tupelo is Paul's scarlet hawthorn (*Crataegus laevigata* 'Paul's Scarlet'). This cultivar appeared as one branch of an English hawthorn in 1858; because it is covered in purple-pink flowers in May, it has become the most popularly planted hawthorn.

EUROPEAN WHITE BIRCH Leaving the Savitt Medical Sciences
Building, follow the main walkway toward the street. Flanking
the sidewalk, growing next to the street, are two European
white birches (*Betula pendula*), native to northern Europe.
These trees, with their white bark and slightly weeping habit,
were once very popular in Reno, but they are susceptible to
the bronze birch borer, which has killed many mature trees.
In the last few years, European white birches have seldom
been planted.

13

Lawlor Events Center, the Planetarium, and Benson Garden

Keep a green tree in your heart and perhaps a singing bird will come.

—CHINESE PROVERB

Lawlor Events Center reflects another classical tradition, different from the Greek columns on the lower campus. Here we have a modern version of the Roman Coliseum, built on a higher slope. As we move north from Lawlor, we find more experiments in architecture and horticulture, prompted by the terrain. The Fleischmann Planetarium suggests a parabola rising from the earth or, as one clever wag suggested forty years ago, a whale with a golf ball in its mouth, emerging from the desert.

When these two buildings appeared on the uphill terrain north of the older campus, an unused fragment of land facing Virginia Street offered a challenge. This time, the owners of the Arlington Gardens nursery responded. Dorothy Benson, an alumna from the 1930s, brought her family's botanical skills.

Brewer's Blackbird in blue Atlas cedar tree. This row of blue Atlas cedars, in front of Lawlor Events Center, commemorates the seven astronauts who died in the *Challenger* space shuttle accident in 1986. Photo by Matt Zytkoskee.

Benson Garden in the foreground, planetarium in the background. The small, yellow flowering tree is goldenchain tree. The tall tree at the top of the picture is black cottonwood. Photo by Matt Zytkoskee.

Path in Benson Garden. The two tree-shrubs in the left foreground are birchleaf mountain mahogany. The green bushy trees behind them are Oriental arborvitae. The tree on the right side of the photo is a juniper. Photo by Jack Hursh.

The Fleischmann Planetarium, pre-landscaping, 1961. Photo courtesy of University Archives, University of Nevada, Reno Libraries.

Arbor Day, 1977. *Left to right*: Ed Kleiner (Arboretum Board chair); Max Milam (university president); unknown; Dorothy Benson (UNR alumna); Richard Post (Arboretum Board member). Photo courtesy of University Archives, University of Nevada, Reno Libraries.

This tangle of trees and paths, known as Benson Garden, could have been designed by a mischievous elf set free on a desert setting. A row of paw paw trees, a new one added annually on Arbor Day, provides a border between the parking garage and the planetarium and gardens. Benson Garden's northern sector features a Japanese Cherry Blossom Garden.

Tree Hunt

Benson Garden ⓭, located on the hillside between N. Virginia Street and Fleischmann Planetarium, has a wild feel, with unpaved footpaths threading through a tangle of trees and shrubs. There are about fifty tree species in this garden alone. Even if you struggle to find the trees on this tree hunt, you'll enjoy the feeling that you can get lost in this overgrown hideaway.

ARIZONA CYPRESS Find the car turnaround on the north side of the planetarium. Now find the wide gravel path that skirts the turnaround and planetarium on the downhill (west) side. Take this path south toward Lawlor Events Center. Just below the planetarium on the right side of the path is a group of tall, grayish conifers, which may have whitish, round berries the size of macadamia nuts. These are Arizona cypress (*Cupressus arizonica*). Note that, besides the bigger trees, there are some smaller trees. These are "volunteers" (trees that spontaneously sprouted from the bigger trees' seeds). Also, look at the peeling bark on the trunks and limbs, which are an appealing color combination of orange, gray, and brown.

TREE OF HEAVEN From the Arizona cypresses, continue south on the wide footpath toward Lawlor Events Center. On the right, between the path and the grassy knoll, are two compound-leaved trees with twenty to thirty leaflets. This is tree of heaven (*Ailanthus altissima*), native to China. This tree has abundant pink seeds and looks good as a landscape tree, but it has a distressing characteristic: it root-suckers easily and can form thickets if not controlled. Perhaps you can spot some volunteer trees sprouting up nearby. Because of its invasive tendencies, the tree of heaven—sometimes called the "tree of hell"—is now on a list of prohibited trees that may no longer be planted on campus.

GOLDENCHAIN TREE From the tree of heaven, make a sharp right on the smaller footpath that skirts the grassy knoll. About 30 yards north of the trail junction, next to the path (under a towering cottonwood tree) on the right is a small tree by itself. This is goldenchain tree (*Laburnum* x *watereri*), a crossbreed between two species of *Laburnum* native to Europe. It has 2-inch leaves divided into three leaflets, reminiscent of clover, long, drooping strings of bright-yellow flowers reminiscent of those of pea, and long, stringy seedpods. All parts of this plant are poisonous, so don't eat it!

14

Cherry Blossom Garden

I think that I shall never see a poem lovely as a tree.

—JOYCE KILMER, "TREES"

Up N. Virginia Street from Benson Garden, west of the Parking Services Building, is the Japanese Cherry Blossom Garden. This garden features many types of flowering cherries—Japanese flowering cherry, weeping Yoshino cherry, weeping Higan cherry, Kwanzan cherry, and Mount Fuji cherry—as well as crabapple, sunburst honey locust, horsetails, and ornamental grasses. In spring a gentle breeze wafts through the flowering trees, unleashing a petal-storm of pinks and whites that flutter down like confetti to settle on the bright-green grass.

The Japanese characters of this arch translate to "Cherry Blossom Garden." Photo by Matt Zytkoskee.

Close-up of a weeping Higan cherry. The horizontal lines (lenticels) on the smooth bark of the tree trunk are characteristic of cherry trees.

Cherry Blossom Garden, with crabapple flowering in springtime.

Fun and frolic in the Cherry Blossom Garden.
Photo by Matt Zytkoskee.

Pond in Cherry Blossom Garden. The tree that dropped
many green leaves in the foreground is the Nevada State
Champion European ash. Photo by Jack Hursh.

The Cherry Blossom Garden was created in memory of Akiko Yamashita by her mother, Kiyoko, and in honor of Hasan Cebi. Akiko was a Japanese student at the university from 1989 to 1996, and Hasan was a Turkish student here from 1988 to 1990. This garden was dedicated in 1999 and later expanded and rededicated in 2012 by the Japanese consul in San Francisco. The Yoshino cherry was a gift from the Japanese consul to commemorate the one-hundredth anniversary of the Washington, DC Tidal Basin trees. Japanese-style arches frame the north and east entrances to this peaceful retreat.

The Benson and Cherry Blossom Gardens are located a mile north of Mackay Quad and uphill from the Hill. As aesthetic counterpoints to the Joe Robertson section of the Fleischmann Agriculture Quad, these two northern gardens have rescued a neglected slope and turned it into a botanical adventure.

Tree Hunt

 The Cherry Blossom Garden **14**, site of this north-campus tree hunt, is across 16th Street from the Nevada Historical Society, and between the university Parking Services Building and N. Virginia Street.

UMBRELLA CATALPA If you go to the southeast corner of the intersection of N. Virginia Street and 16th Street, the umbrella catalpa will be unmistakable as it resembles a super-sized toadstool. The round-headed umbrella catalpa (*Catalpa bignonioides* 'Nana') is a cultivar of the southeastern U.S. native. This grafted cultivar, introduced in the 1880s, produces an umbrella shape and does not have flowers.

RUSSIAN OLIVE In the area with various shrubs and perennials south of the umbrella catalpa is Russian olive (*Elaeagnus angustifolia*), native to southern Europe and central and western Asia. This tree is not really an olive, though its light, silver-green leaves are a similar color. It has nasty thorns and is used as a windbreak or for erosion control. This tree, once established, is extremely drought-tolerant.

WEEPING HIGAN CHERRY Enter the Cherry Blossom Garden and stand on the little wooden bridge. To the north of the bridge (toward the Nevada Historical Society), you'll see a bench. Behind the bench is weeping Higan cherry (*Prunus subhirtella* 'Pendula Plena Rosea'), a weeping cultivar of the species native to Japan. These trees are grafted at about 5 feet to provide a weeping form. It has double pink flowers, and in good years it has bright-yellow fall color.

15

Valley Road Research Garden and Grove

The creation of a thousand forests is in one acorn.

—RALPH WALDO EMERSON, "HISTORY"

A mile east of the main campus on Valley Road is the oldest university farm, sixty acres devoted primarily to greenhouses and a horse stable. A couple of acres here are within the orbit of the Arboretum Board.

In this small grove are about thirty trees planted between 1982 and 1984 as a test of new varieties mostly not native to the region. One can examine species such as the Mondale pine, chestnut oak, pin oak, sawtooth oak, copper beech, weeping Nootka cedar, and Hopa crabapple, in addition to a variety of shrubs.

Now, more than thirty years after planting, this easily overlooked emerald refuge, which lies just south of the Nevada Department of Wildlife

Valley Road Research Garden and Grove. The squat, multi-trunked tree at left is Hopa crabapple; the tall deciduous tree to its right is northern red oak; the pine trees at right are Austrian pines. Photo by Matt Zytkoskee.

Cutting alfalfa at the Valley Road farm, 1929. Photo courtesy
of University Archives, University of Nevada, Reno Libraries.

Valley Road Research Garden and Grove. The two prominent trees
in this photo are sawtooth oak (at left) and giant sequoia (at center).
Photo by Matt Zytkoskee.

Bur oak leaves and acorn, one of
many species of oak at the Valley
Road Research Garden and Grove.

Aspen trunk and daisies, Valley
Road Research Garden and Grove.
Photo by Matt Zytkoskee.

(NDOW), is a little-known hideaway where visitors can picnic on the grass
in the shade amidst an intriguing assortment of mature and oddball trees.
Here horticulture merges with aesthetics. A new strip of pollinator-friendly
native plants along the Valley Road curbside south of the grove promises
to add splashes of color in the future.

Tree Hunt

You may want to drive to the location of this tree hunt, but it will be
a delight to discover this shady retreat with some very cool tree
species. The Valley Road Research Garden **15** is approximately
one mile east of the main campus, at the intersection of Valley Road and
Poplar Street, between the Nevada Department of Wildlife and the University
of Nevada, Biotechnology and Natural Resources Building.

QUAKING ASPEN Along the northwest fringe of the
park, next to the NDOW parking lot, is a two-trunked,
light-barked tree. This is quaking aspen (*Populus
tremuloides*), the most widely distributed broadleaf
tree in the United States. The "quaking" of the leaves
is caused by the connection between the leaf and
the branch, which allows the leaf to turn in the wind.
This tree has reliable yellow fall color; some trees have
orange fall color. It sends out root suckers all around
the tree (cloning itself) and makes thickets. This is why
one particular aspen stand, nicknamed "Pando," in the
Wasatch Mountains of Utah is said to be the largest
organism on Earth.

ROCKY MOUNTAIN BRISTLECONE PINE To the east of the aspen, in the
northern part of the park near NDOW, is a dark, fairly short, round-topped pine
with five short, fat needles in a bundle. This is Rocky Mountain bristlecone
pine (*Pinus aristata*). It is a native of the western United States between the
Rockies and western Utah. Ironically, though not native to Nevada, it is one
of two Nevada state trees, because Rocky Mountain bristlecone pine and
Great Basin bristlecone pine were thought to be
one species when the state tree designation was
made. One difference between the two is that Rocky
Mountain bristlecone pine—and this one is no
exception—has tiny white pitch flecks. If you touch
them, be forewarned: the pitch will not come off until
you wash your hands.

FREMONT COTTONWOOD The large tree in the northeast corner of the park is
Fremont cottonwood (*Populus fremontii*), one of five species of poplar growing
on campus. Native to northern Nevada, this tree grows
rapidly but has weak wood and is subject to pests.
As a result, it has an average lifespan of only about one
hundred years. The largest tree in Nevada is a Fremont
cottonwood nicknamed *el viejo*, or "the old one," located
south of Reno.

A State Arboretum for Nevada

He who plants a tree plants a hope.

—LUCY LARCOM, "PLANT A TREE"

T he idea of establishing a designated arboretum at the university had
been floating like pollen in the Washoe Zephyr for many years before
it actually came to pass. The initial idea for a Nevada state arboretum was
proposed by Professor Edgar Kleiner in 1969, shortly after he was hired
at the University of Nevada, Reno to teach environmental science and
horticulture. Kleiner had earned his master's and doctorate degrees at the
University of Utah during the years when that campus was going through
the process of becoming a state arboretum. When he arrived in Reno,
Kleiner told the chair of the biology department, Dr. Hugh Mozingo, that
Nevada was one of the only states that lacked an arboretum. As Kleiner
recalls,

Dick Post (*left*), second
Arboretum Board chair;
Ed Kleiner (*right*), founder
of the arboretum and first
Arboretum Board chair.

I said, "Hugh, don't you think we ought to get something going to maybe establish an arboretum, a state arboretum? Have the University of Nevada, Reno campus declared the state arboretum?"

He said, "Yeah, let's go over and talk to Edd." The president at that time, of course, was Edd Miller. This was the era of the great Edd Miller presidency.

So the next morning Hugh and I trotted over to Clark Administration, upstairs to the president's office, and sat down with Edd, who said, "I think that's a good idea. Let's form a committee and get things rolling. Ed Kleiner, you are chairman. Hugh, you're on the committee. You two get your heads together and get another few people on your committee. Maybe go over to Ag, knock on some doors."

It would take another fifteen years for the dream of a Nevada state arboretum to be realized, but in the meantime by-laws were written, and a planting and tree labeling program got off the ground. The original arboretum committee eventually became the Arboretum Board, whose mission is to plan university landscape, conduct research, and educate the public.

Several arboretum bills were drafted in the decade after 1975, often long and wordy essays, which were unsuccessful. In 1985, the pattern changed. A crucial participant on the Arboretum Board, becoming its chair in 1983, was Anne Amaral, a librarian. Anne had served in the Nevada State Library in Carson City before coming to the University of Nevada, Reno's Life and Health Sciences library, carrying some of her political experience with her.

An important part of the strategy was to enlist southern Nevada librarian activists in the cause. When that partnership emerged, a successful arboretum bill was crafted.

Here is the text of the bill that was passed on May 14, 1985, and amended slightly in 1993 by the Nevada State Legislature:

State Arboretum
NRS 527.330. Establishment and purpose; regulations.

1. The Board of Regents of the University of Nevada shall establish a state arboretum at each of the universities within the Nevada System of Higher Education to increase the knowledge and appreciation of the public of flora indigenous to Nevada and from other areas and to provide a place where they may be planted and cultivated as memorials.

2. The Board of Regents shall adopt regulations for the establishment and maintenance of the arboreta.

(Added to NRS by 1985, 652; A 1993, 412)

Commemorative tree plantings. *Left*: Donor Carol Ort and Cheryll Glotfelty with white dogwood, 2017. *Right*: Marty Sillito, Jason Lynn, Abram Knight, Raymond Needham, and donor Chris Henry with Autumn Blaze maple, 2016. Left photo by Brandon Hill.

Davene Kaplan, university horticulturist and Arboretum Board member from 1983 to 1995.

This bill was more concise than the previous bills proposed to the legislature, and it carried a fiscal note assuring that no additional appropriation was necessary. Governor Richard Bryan, a University of Nevada, Reno alumnus, signed the bill in 1985. At the university, the Department of Buildings and Grounds had maintenance responsibilities; the Arboretum Board provided essential guidance.

A new kind of university laboratory was underway one hundred years after the campus's founding. Tree planting and removal had been carried out for many decades with little planning, except on the main Quad. A more scientific and aesthetic approach sprouted with the passage of the law. The Arboretum Board has offered advice on improvements, planting, pest control, soil fertility, and trimming. It has organized Arbor Day events and promoted fundraising for the greening of the campus.

Early Arboretum Board chairs and their successors helped develop the university arboretum. But there is another unsung hero who deserves honorable mention in this story. Davene Kaplan earned her MS degree in plant science, working with Professor Wayne Johnson. In 1983 she was hired by the university as horticulturist and worked for the next thirteen years for the university's Buildings and Grounds Services. Davene served on the Arboretum Board from 1983 to 1995. As a certified arborist she procured, planted, and designed landscapes, prizing both beauty and biodiversity. She also ran and maintained records for the Memorial Tree Program, described below. She organized annual Arbor Day celebrations,

Memorial Tree Program plaques (1974–1991), removed in 2016 due to aging.

Arboretum Board members installing the first batch of botanical tree markers, 2016.

Tree marker for star magnolia, one of fifty botanical tree markers installed in 2016.

STAR MAGNOLIA
Magnolia stellata
Magnolia family (Magnoliaceae)
This hardy tree has showy, fragrant white flowers with 12 to 18 petals, large hairy buds, dark green leaves, and striking gray bark. Star magnolia grows to 15–20' tall and 10–15' wide.
ARBORETUM

designed *Tree Walk* brochures, and wrote a weekly column for the staff newspaper about the various types of trees and plants on campus. When Dutch elm disease struck the elms around the old part of campus, Davene worked diligently to remove and replace infected trees. Her prompt action prevented the disease from spreading and possibly wiping out all of the elms on the main Quad. During her years of service, Davene and her staff planted over five hundred trees.

MEMORIAL TREE PROGRAM

From 1974 to 1991 the Arboretum Board ran a successful Memorial Tree Program, which greatly diversified the number of tree species on campus. Under this program, donors could choose from a list of desired tree species. Their donation made it possible for the Arboretum Board to purchase the chosen tree, plant it in a suitable location, and erect an attractive wooden memorial post with a brass-colored plaque that identified the tree species and named the donor and the person in whose honor the tree was planted. Over its lifespan, this program planted more than 120 memorial trees representing nearly 100 different species, including such prizes as the Japanese snowbell, the Bosnian redcone pine, a contorted filbert, and a row of ginkgos. Without the Memorial Tree Program, the university's arboretum would not be as beautiful, interesting, and educational as it is today.

Over the next quarter-century, the Memorial wooden posts and plaques weathered to the point where they became unattractive and in some cases illegible. In 2016 the posts were removed, and new, steel tree stakes with aluminum plaques were installed, providing botanical and landscape information for selected trees in the arboretum. (Memorial Tree records are available in Appendix C.)

In 2015 the university established a Commemorative Tree Program, which once again affords donors the opportunity to support the arboretum by planting a tree to honor a colleague, friend, or loved one. Thanks to the digital age, commemorative information is preserved and available on the University of Nevada, Reno Arboretum's website.

From the 1970s to 1997, the Arboretum Board printed fifteen *Tree Walk* leaflets, guides to identify the greenery in specific areas. Some are still helpful to the neophyte, but many have become too old to be reliable in 2017.

Replacing the old *Tree Walk* brochures, the Arboretum Board in 2017 published twenty-eight self-guided audio tree tours, available on the "Rod's Tree Tours" web page of the University of Nevada, Reno Arboretum website. These tours were created by Arboretum Board member and coauthor of this book, Rod Haulenbeek, aka "The Tree Hunter." Each fifteen- to twenty-minute tour explores a particular area of campus and provides botanical information for about twenty trees. Together, the tours cover all of campus and feature 234 kinds of trees, including 178 species.

Tree Hunt

The trees on this hunt grow near the Clark Administration Building **16**. It was in the president's office of Clark that President Edd Miller approved Ed Kleiner's idea to ask the state legislature to designate the University of Nevada, Reno campus a Nevada State Arboretum.

TULIPTREE Go to the northeast corner of the Clark Administration Building and note the large tree next to the building. This is tuliptree (*Liriodendron tulipifera*, planted 1986). This eastern North America native, which can grow to be the tallest native tree there, is called "tuliptree" because both the leaves and the orange-and-green flowers are shaped like tulip flowers. Its leaves easily identify a tuliptree.

NORTHERN RED OAK Now walk toward Manzanita Lake to the northwest corner of the Clark Administration Building, and notice a large oak tree on the sloping lawn near a short, concrete staircase. This is northern red oak (*Quercus rubra*, planted late 1980s), a native of eastern North America. It is the flagship species of the red oak group, which is characterized by points on each lobe. The northern red oak is perhaps the best oak for this area: it has reliably good fall color, is relatively trouble-free, and grows quickly. This tree was planted to honor Joe Crowley, who served as the University of Nevada, Reno president for twenty-three years, from 1978 to 2001.

JEFFREY PINE From the outside stairs by the northwest corner of the Clark Administration Building, look toward Manzanita Lake. Just across the walking path, opposite a bike rack, you'll see a tall pine tree. This conifer with long needles in bunches of three is Jeffrey pine (*Pinus jeffreyi*). It is native to the Sierra Nevada and is the most populous tree on the eastern flank. Some people have problems distinguishing between Jeffrey pine and the similar-looking ponderosa pine. Ponderosa pine has small, fist-sized cones and its bark has no smell, while Jeffrey pine has 6-inch cones, and its bark smells to most people like vanilla. Ponderosa cones feel prickly to hold in your hand ("prickly ponderosa"), while Jeffrey cones are painless to hold ("gentle Jeffrey"). Both pines were logged for the Comstock silver boom in nearby Virginia City, and as a result the Lake Tahoe Basin was severely deforested. The pines that grow there now are second- and third-growth.

Tree Campus USA

Other holidays repose upon the past; Arbor Day proposes for the future.

—J. STERLING MORTON

When the state legislature made the decision in 1885 to move the fledgling university from Elko to Reno, the Board of Regents considered several cities before it selected the Hill. It bought the initial ten acres from John N. Evans, who owned a ranch north of the town, and laid the foundations of Morrill Hall the same year.

Ceremony celebrating the university's first year as Tree Campus USA, 2015 (for eligibility met in 2014). *Left to right*: Ed Kleiner (founder of the arboretum); David Howlett (Nevada Division of Forestry); Marc Johnson (university president); Cheryll Glotfelty (Arboretum Board chair); Marty Sillito (assistant director of Grounds Services). Photo by Theresa Danna-Douglas.

The first Arbor Day celebration at the University of Nevada,
Reno, 1904. Photo courtesy of the Nevada Historical Society.

Arbor Day 2017 tree planting. The tree is a trident
maple. The woman facing the camera is Mya Yazbek,
president of the university student Plant Club, which
raised money to purchase trees for this event.

Expansion of the campus began almost immediately. It had grown to about forty acres by 1900, expanded to eighty-six acres by 1940, and reached two-hundred-plus acres by 1986, the centenary of the first classes in Morrill Hall. By 2017, with additions mostly to the north, the campus had more than three hundred acres.

The main campus, which we previously described as a goblet, includes about 320 acres. When Facilities and Grounds Services commissioned an inventory in 2014, it identified about 3,500 trees representing 150 species and cultivars. Forty percent of these were conifers—mostly pines—the reliable friends of Great Basin landscapers.

In the broadleaf category, maples, plums, and pears prevailed, constituting 17.6 percent of the trees on campus. The rest of the broadleaf trees diversify so much in species that their number is negligible. For example, ginkgos make up 1 percent or less of the total trees in the broadleaf category.

Student-led tree tour, stopping at a cutleaf weeping birch.

More than 75 percent of all trees were in good condition, reflecting the care given by groundskeepers over the years. Others were recommended for additional care or removal.

Between 2014 and 2017, approximately twenty-five new tree species were planted on campus with the help of student and Arboretum Board volunteers. These additions enrich the arboretum's collection, enhance biodiversity, and are an experiment to see what tree species will thrive in Reno's high-desert environment.

In 2014 the University of Nevada, Reno was recognized as a Tree Campus USA through a program sponsored by the National Arbor Day Foundation. Tree Campus USA designation honors colleges and universities for establishing and sustaining healthy community forests along with promoting student involvement. Universities must meet five standards, including having a campus tree advisory committee, a tree care plan, annual expenditures dedicated to the tree program, an Arbor Day observance, and a service-learning project.

In 2016 the university won the Grand Award from the Professional Grounds Management Society. This award recognizes exceptional grounds maintenance. Marty Sillito, Assistant Director of Grounds Services, said,

> I believe we won the award, in part, because of some of our large-scale green waste diversion, green waste recycling, and all-natural soil fertility projects. The all-organic composted products that the university purchases for its lawns and gardens reduce the reliance on chemical pesticides and herbicides. Our campus landscape also provides a variety of attractive features, such as waterfalls, wisteria-covered trellises, creeping vines, blooming rose gardens, a wide variety of daffodils, tulips, irises, and hyacinth, and a beautifully manicured lawn on the historic Quad, which is listed on the National Register of Historic Places and surrounded by century-old elms.

Tree Hunt

 This tour explores trees in the newer part of campus. It starts in front of the Fitzgerald Student Services Building 17 .

ARISTOCRAT PEAR   The trees in the grassy circle in front of the Fitzgerald Student Services Building are aristocrat pear (*Pyrus calleryana* 'Aristocrat'). The species is native to Japan and Korea. This is a cultivar of callery pear, probably the second-most-planted tree in northern Nevada because it is truly a three-season tree: in spring it has abundant white flowers, in summer it has glossy, dark-green, smooth-edged leaves, and in fall it has bright colors that can range from yellow to orange to red to purple (depending on the tree and the fall weather). This cultivar has an open form. On the downside, the limbs of this tree are prone to breakage, and some people dislike the smell of its flowers.

EUROPEAN MOUNTAIN ASH   From the Fitzgerald Student Services Building, head toward the Knowledge Center, but stop before you reach the crosswalk. In a trapezoidal grassy area with manhole covers and a utility box, you'll see two planter circles, out of which grow medium-sized, compound-leaved trees. These are European mountain ash (*Sorbus aucuparia*, planted 2000). This species is native to Europe, western Asia, and Siberia. In some cases, it has escaped cultivation and is growing wild. It is valued for its orange-red fall color and its orange or red berries, which hang on all winter.

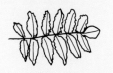

GOLDENRAIN TREE   From the Fitzgerald Student Services Building, cross the street at the crosswalk and proceed past the big blue "N" sign to the semicircular, concrete courtyard by the lower southwest entrance to the Knowledge Center. Here you'll find several sculptures, some benches, and three compound-leaved trees. These are goldenrain trees (*Koelreuteria paniculata*, planted 2008), native to China, Japan, and Korea. It is a three-season tree: in early summer, after the other trees have bloomed, it has cylinders of small yellow flowers; its lantern-shaped fruit starts out green, turns to yellow in fall, turns brown in winter and stays on the tree until the leaves come out the next spring. The pea-sized black seeds that lurk inside the lantern can be drilled and strung into a necklace.

The Future

As an instrument of planetary home repair,
it is hard to imagine anything as safe as a tree.

—JONATHAN WEINER

In 2017, the university was in the process of acquiring lots in the residential area south of campus, down from the Hill toward the city. That zone has been largely older residential dwellings.

The *Campus Master Plan 2015–2024* expects the campus to expand southward, absorbing the blocks between the Hill and Interstate 80 and, eventually, some blocks south of the freeway. If this were to happen, what would be the impact on the serenity of the lower campus?

Artistic rendering of the future of the University of Nevada, Reno from the *Campus Master Plan, 2015–2024*. The freeway that cuts diagonally in the lower right is I-80. High rises, a shopping area, and a new campus entrance are planned for the blocks between I-80 and the main campus. Existing trees and landscape on the Ninth Street hill will be preserved. Courtesy of University of Nevada, Reno.

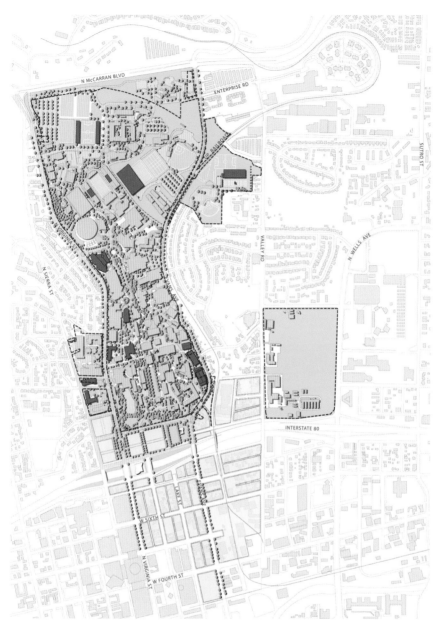

Map from the *Campus Master Plan, 2015–2024*, showing plans for university expansion south of I-80. Courtesy of University of Nevada, Reno.

A venerable cluster of trees on campus stands on the slope south of Morrill Hall, where the Hill falls sharply to the Ninth Street base of the goblet. Here is the oldest, most majestic, and least disturbed sector of the arboretum. Fortunately, this verdant slope is master-planned to remain a green natural area, providing habitat for birds as well as beauty and a sense of well-being for people who approach campus from the south.

Plans for a new campus entrance at N. Virginia Street and Ninth Street from the *Campus Master Plan, 2015–2024*. Courtesy of University of Nevada, Reno.

Aerial looking south, with the university campus in the foreground and the City of Reno in the background. Interstate 80 runs east-west (left to right) in the center of the photo. The university plans to expand across I-80 in the coming decades. Photo courtesy of University of Nevada, Reno.

At the north rim, below the North McCarran ring road, hillsides of sagebrush, rabbitbrush, and other native groundcover remain, reminiscent of the foliage that dominated the Hill 130 years ago.

But the north campus has some catching up to do. The *Master Plan* observes that

> The University over decades of growth has not emulated the pedestrian and shaded quality first established for the campus more than 100 years ago. Walking north from the historic quad, the campus tree cover diminishes as does the quality of the pedestrian experience. The role of landscape in creating comfortable, low-water use campus settings is critical to the success of the campus plan. Planting trees throughout campus to benefit the pedestrian experience and lower ambient temperature should be an ongoing effort as the campus grows and evolves.

The plan targets the northern Bio-Medical Precinct especially as an area in need of more tree cover. Along the west and east sides of the campus goblet, in order to promote a pedestrian-friendly environment, the plan specifies that streets, including N. Virginia Street and Evans Avenue, include generous sidewalks on both sides of the street that are shaded with street trees.

For those who love trees, it is reassuring that the official vision for the university's future recognizes the many benefits that urban trees provide. According to research findings indexed and made available by the Arbor Day Foundation, urban trees help clean our air and water, provide cooling, save energy, benefit wildlife, reduce crime, increase property values, and contribute to our health. Perhaps less quantifiable, trees nourish the soul.

The Nevada State Champion eastern cottonwood, growing on the Ninth Street hill. This tree has witnessed many changes over the last century and, with any luck, will witness many more. Photo by Matt Zytkoskee.

Tree Hunt

The location for this tree hunt—the northeast corner of the intersection of Ninth Street and Center Street ⓲—is easy to find as there is a prominent cluster of tall evergreens crowded together at the corner. To the casual observer these trees might look like "a bunch of pine trees." Not so! What we have here is an interesting mix of spruces and firs.

SPANISH FIR The tree on the very corner of the conifer group at Ninth Street and Center Street is Spanish fir (*Abies pinsapo*, probably planted about 1950). A native of Spain, it looks to most people like a spruce because it has fat needles. However, its cones are egg-shaped and upright; in contrast, spruce cones grow downward. The needles are soft, unlike the sharp spruce needles. The branches grow level or upright. This tree is the Nevada State Champion.

WHITE SPRUCE If you stay on Center Street, immediately to the left of the Spanish fir—the second tree from the corner—is white spruce (*Picea glauca*, probably planted around 1950), native to the northern United States and southern Canada. This spruce has 2-inch cones that hang down from   the branches. White spruces dwarf well: there are many dwarf cultivars on the market, including the dwarf Alberta spruce, which looks like a pointed gumdrop decorating the campus cake. White spruce branches grow level or upward. There are only two of these trees on campus, and this is the Nevada State Champion.

CANDICANS WHITE FIR From the intersection of Ninth Street and Center Street, walk east on the Ninth Street sidewalk and notice the two gray-green conifers that stand behind the Spanish fir. These are Candicans white firs (*Abies concolor* 'Candicans'). White fir is native to the Sierra Nevada and makes up about a third of the trees in the Lake Tahoe area. It is identified by upright cones on the top fourth of the tree, and by flat needles that stick out perpendicular to the branch. The 'Candicans' cultivar differs from the species in that its needles are larger and are silver-gray.

Commencement

Today I have grown taller from walking with the trees.

—KARLE WILSON BAKER, "GOOD COMPANY"

The university's annual commencement ceremony in May takes place on the historic main Quad, ringed by enormous elm trees. These sheltering elms provide welcome shade to the throng of graduates and families, and their tall trunks and towering branches send an uplifting message to graduates to reach for their dreams.

University of Nevada alumni, returning during Homecoming week for their ten, twenty-five, and even fifty-year reunions, visit the Quad and other parts of campus, where memories of their years as college students are gently triggered by the trees.

The impulse to plant a tree must be as old as civilization. Tending saplings is probably a primordial instinct. The inclination to cultivate a grove for aesthetic purposes—the search for natural beauty in a planned context—is more recent.

Commencement ceremony on the main Quad, May 2016.

Commencement 1908 at the main Quad, north of Morrill Hall. The president's house is at left. Photo courtesy of University Archives, University of Nevada, Reno Libraries.

Arboretum Board student representative Kirsten Schuhmacher, showing the arboretum spirit, May 2017.

Jim Hulse—University of Nevada, Reno alumnus, history professor emeritus, and coauthor of this guide—strolling under the elms along the main Quad (*top*). Photo by Jack Hursh.

Pink dogwood flowers (*left*). Photo by Jean Dixon.

Farewell! Come back soon (*right*). Photo by Matt Zytkoskee.

An arboretum is more than an occasional tree planting. It might be a botanical tapestry within the context of an urban university. It is a learning experience and a microcosm of human efforts to cultivate small sections of the planet for plants, rather than to exploit every corner for bricks and mortar. In a university setting, an arboretum is a partner in the learning laboratory and a short sabbatical for all who stroll there.

Tree Hunt

This concluding tree hunt commences on the east side of the main Quad between the Paul Laxalt Mineral Engineering Building and the Mackay Science Building **19**. If the university's commencement ceremony were underway, these trees would be directly behind the main stage.

PINK FLOWERING DOGWOOD Growing at the northwest corner of the Mackay Science Building is a small tree in a planter bed next to the building. This is pink flowering dogwood (*Cornus florida*, could be any of a number of cultivars). Flowering dogwood is native to eastern North America, and its small size and abundant cross-shaped flowers result in its being planted in millions of yards across North America.

COMMON HORSE-CHESTNUT Standing prominently at the southwest corner of the Paul Laxalt Mineral Engineering Building is a tree with five leaflets on each palmately compound leaf. This is common horse-chestnut (*Aesculus hippocastanum*), native to mountainous wilds of Greece and Albania. In spring it has large striking clusters of white flowers, followed in fall by spiny fruits. The seeds inside are round, reddish brown, and about an inch in diameter and look like those of the near-relative American chestnut. However, they require special preparation to be easily digestible. Common horse-chestnut is widely planted in park areas of Europe, where the trees are shaped (some might say "mutilated").

PAPERBARK BIRCH Take the sidewalk between the Paul Laxalt Mineral Engineering Building and the Mackay Science Building toward the Paul Laxalt Mineral Research Building tucked behind them. Along the sidewalk to your left, a few feet past a stairway and a door, is a tree with white bark. This is the Nevada State "Up-and-Coming Tree" paperbark birch (*Betula papyrifera,* planted 1989). Native to eastern and midwestern North America, it has the greatest geographical distribution of any native birch. It is also called canoe birch. Because the bark is weather-resistant and the wood is soft, Indians carved out the soft wood and made canoes out of this tree. One of its less-dramatic uses today is for Popsicle sticks.

APPENDIX A

Tree Species and Cultivars at the University of Nevada, Reno

Compiled by Rod Haulenbeek

To understand the list of tree species and cultivars at the university, it will be helpful to know some key terms.

Scientific Name

People in different regions may call the same tree by different "common names." For example, Douglas fir has over twenty common names. Almost three hundred years ago, Carl Linnaeus devised a system of scientific nomenclature to avoid this confusion. The first part of the scientific name, a Latin name in italics, refers to the genus. For example, the genus of Douglas fir is *Pseudotsuga* ("false hemlock"). To further classify the plant, a species name is used, also in italics. In many cases, the species name tells something about the plant. For example, *Acer macrophyllum* refers to a maple (*Acer*) with large leaves (*macro*, meaning "large," and *phylum*, meaning "leaf").

Hybrid

A hybrid is an offspring of two different plant species. The standard notation for hybrids is an "x" between the genus and species names. An example of a hybrid on campus is London planetree (*Platanus* x *acerifolia*), the offspring of American sycamore (*Platanus occidentalis*) and Oriental planetree (*Platanus orientalis*). In this case, hybridization apparently occurred accidentally with parent trees in close proximity around 1683 in England. Hybridization today is a multibillion-dollar business, as plant breeders attempt to improve attributes of plants. For example, *Quercus* x *warei* is a hybrid of columnar English oak (*Quercus robur* 'Fastigiata') and swamp white oak (*Quercus bicolor*); the offspring has improved tolerance to cold and disease.

Cultivar

A cultivar is a *culti*vated *vari*ant of a species. The standard notation for cultivars is single quotes, with the cultivar name nonitalicized. Cultivars may occur as a result of cross-pollination, natural variation, or from buds or cuttings grafted from one kind of plant to another. Cultivars may not reproduce true from seed (e.g., seeds from a weeping cherry, if planted, may not produce another weeping cherry).

The cultivar is marketed for a certain trait, such as flower color (spring snow crabapple, scientific name *Malus* 'Spring Snow'), tree size or shape (weeping Norway spruce, scientific name *Picea abies* 'Pendula'), or disease resistance (several cultivars of Dutch elm are resistant to Dutch elm disease). Cultivars are given "plant patents" similar to other patents, for example, U.S. Plant Patent PP12,673 for 'Long,' a cultivar of the hybrid *Quercus* x *warei.* The plant breeder has rights to the cultivar, and others are forbidden to propagate the cultivar for sale, or the plant breeder gets a royalty. Plant patent lives vary, but twenty-five to thirty years is the common length.

Variety

A variety is a different-looking form of the same species, both forms occurring naturally in the wild. The standard notation for a variety is the nonitalicized "var" between the species name and the variety name. Seeds of the variety will be true to the parent. One example on campus is the thornless honey-locust (*Gleditsia triacanthos* var. *inermis*), a thornless variety of honey locust (*Gleditsia triacanthos*).

Those who wish to locate every tree variety on campus will find a Rosetta stone on the "Rod's Tree Tours" link of the UNR Arboretum website. There, on Rod's comprehensive list of tree species, you can look up a particular tree species and find out which of the twenty-eight self-guided tree tours includes that species.

TREE SPECIES AND CULTIVARS AT THE UNIVERSITY OF NEVADA, RENO

Trees uncommon in the Reno–Sparks area are indicated in **bold**

Common Name	Scientific Name
Alder, European or Black	***Alnus glutinosa***
Alder, Mountain	***Alnus tenuifolia***
Alder, White	***Alnus rhombifolia***
Apple	*Malus domestica*
Arborvitae, Eastern	*Thuja occidentalis*
Arborvitae, Oriental	*Thuja orientalis*
Ash, Autumn Purple	*Fraxinus americana* 'Autumn Purple'
Ash, Black	***Fraxinus nigra***
Ash, European	***Fraxinus excelsior***
Ash, Green	*Fraxinus pennsylvanica*
Ash, Narrowleaf	***Fraxinus angustifolia***
Ash, Oregon	***Fraxinus latifolia***
Ash, Patmore	*Fraxinus pennsylvanica* 'Patmore'
Ash, Raywood	*Fraxinus oxycarpa* 'Raywood'
Ash, Summit	***Fraxinus pennsylvanica* 'Summit'**
Ash, Velvet	***Fraxinus velutina***
Aspen, Quaking	*Populus tremuloides*
Beech, European	*Fagus sylvatica*
Beech, Tricolor	***Fagus sylvatica* 'Tricolor'**
Beech, Weeping European	***Fagus sylvatica* 'Pendula'**
Birch, Cutleaf Weeping	*Betula pendula* 'Laciniata'
Birch, European White	*Betula pendula*
Birch, Paperbark	***Betula papyrifera***
Birch, River	*Betula nigra*
Birch, Water	***Betula occidentalis***
Birch, Young's Weeping	***Betula pendula* 'Youngii'**
Buckeye, Arnold	***Aesculus x arnoldiana* 'Autumn Splendor'**
Buckeye, Ohio	***Aesculus glabra***
Catalpa, Northern or Western	*Catalpa speciosa*
Catalpa, Umbrella	***Catalpa bignonoides* 'Nana'**
Cedar of Lebanon	***Cedrus libani***
Cedar, Blue Atlas	*Cedrus atlantica* 'Glauca'
Cedar, Deodar	*Cedrus deodara*

Common Name	Scientific Name
Cedar, Nootka or Alaska	***Callitropsis nootkatensis***
Cedar, Port Orford	***Chamaecyparis lawsoniana***
Cedar, Weeping Atlas	*Cedrus atlantica* 'Glauca Pendula'
Cedar, Weeping Deodar	***Cedrus deodara* 'Prostrate Beauty'**
Cedar, Weeping Nootka or Alaska	***Callitropsis nootkatensis* 'Pendula'**
Cedar, Western Red	*Thuja plicata*
Cherry, Fruiting	*Prunus avium*
Cherry, Japanese Flowering	*Prunus serrulata*
Cherry, Kwanzan	*Prunus serrulata* 'Kwanzan'
Cherry, Mount Fuji	***Prunus serrulata* 'Shirotae'**
Cherry, Purple-Leaf Sand	*Prunus x cistena*
Cherry, Shogetsu	***Prunus serrulata* 'Shogetsu'**
Cherry, Snow Fountains	*Prunus* 'Snofozam'
Cherry, Weeping Higan	*Prunus subhirtella* 'Pendula Plena Rosea'
Chestnut, Colossal	***Castanea sativa x crenata***
Chokecherry	*Prunus virginiana*
Chokecherry, Amur	***Prunus maackii***
Chokecherry, Canada Red	*Prunus virginiana* 'Canada Red'
Cottonwood, Black	*Populus trichocarpa*
Cottonwood, Eastern	***Populus deltoides***
Cottonwood, Fremont	*Populus fremontii*
Crabapple	*Malus sp.*
Crabapple, Candied Apple	***Malus* 'Candied Apple'**
Crabapple, Hopa	*Malus* 'Hopa'
Crabapple, Pink Spires	***Malus* 'Pink Spires'**
Crabapple, Red Jade Weeping	***Malus x scheideckeri* 'Red Jade'**
Crabapple, Transcendent	***Malus* 'Transcendent'**
Currant, Golden	*Ribes aureum*
Cypress, Arizona	***Cupressus arizonica***
Cypress, Bald	***Taxodium distichum***
Cypress, Leyland	x *Cuprocyparis leylandii*
Cypress, Weeping Sawara	***Chamaecyparis pisifera* 'Aurea Pendula'**
Dogwood, Cornelian Cherry	***Cornus mas***

Common Name	Scientific Name
Dogwood, Creek	*Cornus sericea*
Dogwood, Flowering	*Cornus florida*
Dogwood, Giant	*Cornus controversa*
Dogwood, Kousa	*Cornus kousa*
Dogwood, Pagoda	*Cornus alternifolia*
Dogwood, Pink Flowering	*Cornus florida* 'Pink'
Elderberry, Blue	***Sambucus caerulea***
Elm	*Ulmus sp.*
Elm, Camperdown	***Ulmus glabra* 'Camperdownii'**
Elm, Dutch	*Ulmus x hollandica*
Elm, European White	***Ulmus laevis***
Elm, Princeton	***Ulmus americana* 'Princeton'**
Elm, Scotch	***Ulmus glabra***
Elm, Siberian	*Ulmus pumila*
Euonymus, Winged	***Euonymus alatus***
Fir, Candicans	*Abies concolor* 'Candicans'
Fir, Douglas	*Pseudotsuga menziesii*
Fir, Spanish	***Abies pinsapo***
Fir, White	*Abies concolor*
Ginkgo	***Ginkgo biloba***
Goldenchain Tree	***Laburnum* x *watereri***
Goldenrain Tree	*Koelreuteria paniculata*
Hackberry, Common	*Celtis occidentalis*
Handkerchief (Dove) Tree	*Davidia involucrata*
Hawthorn, Crimson Cloud	*Crataegus laevigata* 'Crimson Cloud'
Hawthorn, English	*Crataegus laevigata*
Hawthorn, Lavalle	***Crataegus* x *lavallei***
Hawthorn, Paul's Scarlet	*Crataegus laevigata* 'Paul's Scarlet'
Hawthorn, Thornless Cockspur	***Crataegus crus-galli* 'Inermis'**
Hawthorn, Washington	***Crataegus phaenopyrum***
Hawthorn, Winter King	***Crataegus viridris* 'Winter King'**
Hazelnut, Harry Lauder's Walking Stick	***Corylus avellana* 'Tortuosa'**
Hickory, Shagbark	***Carya ovata***
Holly, American	***Ilex opaca***

Common Name	Scientific Name
Holly, English	***Ilex aquifolium***
Holly, Variegated American	*Ilex opaca* 'Variegata'
Honey Locust, Ruby Lace	***Gleditsia triacanthos* var. *inermis* 'Ruby Lace'**
Honey Locust, Sunburst	*Gleditsia triacanthos* var. *inermis* 'Sunburst'
Honey Locust, Thornless	*Gleditsia triacanthos* var. *inermis*
Honeysuckle, Amur	***Lonicera maackii***
Hornbeam, American	***Carpinus caroliniana***
Hornbeam, European	*Carpinus betulus* 'Fastigiata'
Horsechestnut, Common	*Aesculus hippocastanum*
Horsechestnut, Red	***Aesculus x carnea* 'Briotti'**
Incense Cedar	*Calocedrus decurrens*
Joshua Tree	***Yucca brevifolia***
Juniper	*Juniperus sp.*
Juniper, Rocky Mountain	*Juniperus scopulorum*
Juniper, Spartan	***Juniperus* 'Spartan'**
Juniper, Utah	*Juniperus osteosperma*
Katsura Tree	*Cercidiphyllum japonicum*
Katsura Tree, Weeping	*Cercidiphyllum japonicum* 'Pendula'
Kentucky Coffee Tree	***Gymnocladus dioicus***
Larch, Japanese	***Larix kaempferi***
Lilac, Japanese Tree	***Syringa reticulata***
Lilac, Peking (China Snow)	***Syringa reticulata* subsp. *pekinensis* 'China Snow'**
Linden, American Basswood	*Tilia americana*
Linden, Crimean	***Tilia x euchlora***
Linden, Littleleaf	*Tilia cordata*
Linden, Silver	***Tilia tomentosa***
Locust, Black	*Robinia pseudoacacia*
Magnolia, Alexandrina Saucer	***Magnolia x soulangeana* 'Alexandrina'**
Magnolia, Cucumber	***Magnolia acuminata***
Magnolia, Kobus	***Magnolia kobus***
Magnolia, Lennei Saucer	*Magnolia x soulangeana* 'Lennei'
Magnolia, Star	*Magnolia stellata*
Maple, Amur	*Acer ginnala*
Maple, Bigtooth	***Acer grandidentatum***

Common Name	Scientific Name
Maple, Black	***Acer nigrum***
Maple, Bloodgood Japanese	*Acer palmatum* 'Bloodgood'
Maple, Boxelder	*Acer negundo*
Maple, Chalkbark	***Acer leucoderme***
Maple, Columnar Freeman	*Acer x freemanii* 'Marmo'
Maple, Columnar Norway	*Acer platanoides* 'Columnare'
Maple, Columnar Red	*Acer rubrum* 'Columnare'
Maple, Crimson King	*Acer platanoides* 'Crimson King'
Maple, Cutleaf Silver	***Acer saccharinum* 'Laciniatum'**
Maple, Deborah	***Acer platanoides* 'Deborah'**
Maple, Freeman	*Acer x freemanii*
Maple, Japanese	*Acer palmatum*
Maple, Nizetti Sycamore	***Acer pseudoplatanus* 'Nizetti'**
Maple, Norway	*Acer platanoides*
Maple, Paperbark	***Acer griseum***
Maple, Purpleblow	***Acer truncatum***
Maple, Red	*Acer rubrum*
Maple, Schwedler	***Acer platanoides* 'Schwedleri'**
Maple, Silver	*Acer saccharinum*
Maple, Sugar	***Acer saccharum***
Maple, Sycamore	***Acer pseudoplatanus***
Maple, Trident	***Acer buergerianum***
Maple, Vine	*Acer circinatum*
Monkey Puzzle Tree	***Araucaria araucana***
Mountain Ash, European	*Sorbus aucuparia*
Mountain Mahogany, Birchleaf	***Cercocarpus betuloides***
Mountain Mahogany, Curl-Leaf	*Cercocarpus ledifolius*
Mulberry, Fruitless White	*Morus alba* 'Fruitless'
Mulberry, Red	***Morus rubra***
Mulberry, Weeping	***Morus alba* 'Pendula'**
Oak, Bur	*Quercus macrocarpa*
Oak, Chestnut	*Quercus prinus*
Oak, Columnar English	*Quercus robur* 'Fastigiata'
Oak, Dwarf Chinkapin	***Quercus prinoides***
Oak, Northern Red	*Quercus rubra*
Oak, Pin	*Quercus palustris*
Oak, Regal Prince	***Quercus x warei* 'Long'**

Common Name	Scientific Name
Oak, Sawtooth	***Quercus acutissima***
Oak, Scarlet	*Quercus coccinea*
Oak, Shingle	***Quercus imbricaria***
Oak, Shumard	*Quercus shumardii*
Oak, Valley	***Quercus lobata***
Oak, White	***Quercus alba***
Olive, Autumn	***Elaeagnus umbellata***
Olive, Russian	*Elaeagnus angustifolia*
Pagoda Tree, Japanese	***Sophora japonica***
Paw paw	***Asimina triloba***
Pear, Aristocrat	*Pyrus calleryana* 'Aristocrat'
Pear, Bradford	*Pyrus calleryana* 'Bradford'
Pear, Capital	*Pyrus calleryana* 'Capital'
Pear, Chanticleer	*Pyrus calleryana* 'Chanticleer'
Peashrub, Siberian	***Caragana arborescens***
Photinia, Red Tip	*Photinia* x *fraseri*
Pine, Afghan or Mondale	***Pinus eldarica***
Pine, Austrian	*Pinus nigra*
Pine, Bosnian	***Pinus heldreichii* var. leucodermis**
Pine, Columnar Eastern White	***Pinus strobus* 'Fastigiata'**
Pine, Columnar Scotch	***Pinus sylvestris* 'Fastigiata'**
Pine, Contorted Eastern White	***Pinus strobus* 'Contorta'**
Pine, Digger	***Pinus sabiniana***
Pine, Eastern White	***Pinus strobus***
Pine, Japanese Black	***Pinus thunbergii***
Pine, Jeffrey	*Pinus jeffreyi*
Pine, Sierra Lodgepole	***Pinus contorta* var. murrayana**
Pine, Mugo	*Pinus mugo*
Pine, Ponderosa	*Pinus ponderosa*
Pine, Rocky Mountain Bristlecone	***Pinus aristata***
Pine, Scotch	*Pinus sylvestris*
Pine, Shore	***Pinus contorta* var. contorta**
Pine, Single-Leaf Pinyon	*Pinus monophylla*
Pine, Southwestern White or Border	***Pinus strobiformis***
Pine, Sugar	***Pinus lambertiana***

Common Name	Scientific Name
Pine, Two-Needle Pinyon	***Pinus edulis***
Pine, Vanderwolf	*Pinus flexilis* 'Vanderwolf'
Pine, Washoe	***Pinus ponderosa* var. washoensis**
Pine, Weeping Eastern White	***Pinus strobus* 'Pendula'**
Pine, Weeping Japanese Red	***Pinus densiflora* 'Pendula'**
Pine, Western White	***Pinus monticola***
Pistache, Chinese	***Pistacia chinensis***
Pistache, Red Push	***Pistacia chinensis* 'Red Push'**
Plum, Blireana Flowering	***Prunus* x *blireana***
Plum, Purple Leaf	*Prunus cerasifera*
Redbud, Eastern	*Cercis canadensis*
Redbud, Covey Weeping Eastern	***Cercis canadensis* 'Covey'**
Redwood, Coast	***Sequoia sempervirens***
Redwood, Dawn	***Metasequoia glyptostroboides***
Sequoia, Giant	*Sequoiadendron giganteum*
Sequoia, Weeping	*Sequoiadendron giganteum* 'Pendula'
Serviceberry, Autumn Brilliance	***Amelanchier* x *grandiflora* 'Autumn Brilliance'**
Smoketree	*Cotinus coggygria*
Snowbell, Japanese	***Styrax japonicus***
Spindletree, European	***Euonymus europaeus***
Spruce, Colorado Blue	*Picea pungens*
Spruce, Dwarf Alberta	*Picea glauca* 'Conica'
Spruce, Dwarf Colorado Blue	***Picea pungens* 'Fat Albert'**
Spruce, Norway	*Picea abies*
Spruce, Serbian	***Picea omorika***
Spruce, Weeping Norway	***Picea abies* 'Pendula'**
Spruce, Weeping Serbian	***Picea omorika* 'Pendula'**
Spruce, Weeping White	***Picea glauca* 'Pendula'**
Spruce, White	***Picea glauca***
Sumac, Staghorn	*Rhus typhina*
Sumac, Three-Leaf	***Rhus trilobata***
Sweetgum	*Liquidambar styraciflua*
Sweetgum, Worplesdon	***Liquidambar styraciflua* 'Worplesdon'**
Sycamore, American	*Platanus occidentalis*

Common Name	Scientific Name
Sycamore, London Planetree	***Platanus x acerifolia***
Tree of Heaven	*Ailanthus altissima*
Tulip Tree	***Liriodendron tulipifera***
Tupelo	***Nyssa sylvatica***
Walnut, Black	Juglans nigra
Walnut, English	***Juglans regia***
Willow	*Salix sp.*
Willow, Globe	***Salix matsudana* 'Navajo'**
Willow, Weeping	*Salix babylonica*
Willow, Weeping Pussy	***Salix caprea* 'Pendula'**
Yew, English	***Taxus baccata***
Zelkova, Japanese or Sawleaf	***Zelkova serrata***
Species	172
Cultivars	80
Total Kinds of Trees	252
Locally Uncommon Trees	136

APPENDIX B

State Champion Trees at the University of Nevada, Reno

Compiled by Rod Haulenbeek

There is a list of state champion trees for each state in the United States, as well as a list of national champions. To be a state champion, a tree must be the biggest of its kind in the state. Nevada's state champion list can be found by googling "Nevada's Big Tree Program," then linking to "Nevada Big Tree Register."

Championship status is based on a point system, established nationally. Points are awarded as follows:

- 1 point for each inch of circumference at 4.5 feet above ground
- 1 point for each foot of height
- ¼ point for each foot of average crown spread

These three numbers are totaled, and, if the nominated tree has at least 10 points more than the next biggest tree, it is the state champion. "Champions" are the biggest of their kind in the state; "co-champions" are within 10 points of each other.

Almost all tree species in Nevada are introduced. They are generally not as big as trees native to an area and perhaps several hundred years old. For example, the national champion American hornbeam, growing in New Jersey where it is a native species, has 235 points; the largest American hornbeam in Nevada, probably planted in the last twenty years, has only 47 points. In order to acknowledge the efforts of Nevadans to increase species diversity, the Nevada Division of Forestry (which administers the state list) has created a new category, "up-and-coming" tree.

STATE CHAMPION TREES AT THE UNIVERSITY OF NEVADA, RENO

Common Name / Scientific Name	Type of Champion	Location	CBH (inches)	Height (inches)	Spread (inches)	Points
SOUTHEASTERN CAMPUS						
American Holly *Ilex opaca*	Up-and-coming	Corner of Scrugham Engineering 20 ft. W. of underpass	27	35	14	66
Bald Cypress *Taxodium distichum*	Champion	Ag Quad right of sidewalk from 9th St.	60	70	43	141
Black Maple *Acer nigrum*	Up-and-coming	S. side Laxalt Mineral Research Building	30	34	25	70
Chokecherry *Prunus virginiana* 'Canada Red'	Champion	30 ft. E. of N.E. corner Orvis Building	29	38	26	73
Columnar Scotch Pine *Pinus sylvestris* 'Fastigiata'	Up-and-coming	10 ft. from steps and 9th St. sidewalk	28	34	11	65
Crimean Linden *Tilia euchlora*	Champion	Raised planter E. of Orvis Building	24	37	21	66
Eastern Cottonwood *Populus deltoides*	Champion	Lawn area 50 ft. W. of steps from 9th St.	205	138	83	364
English Holly *Ilex aquifolium*	Champion	S. side of Ag Quad	19	23	17	46
Ginkgo *Ginkgo biloba*	Champion	N.E. corner of Ag Quad	45	62	33	115

Common name / Scientific name	Status	Location				
Japanese Maple *Acer palmatum*	Champion	N. of W. entrance Orvis Building	33	21	34	64
Japanese Pagoda Tree *Sophora japonica*	Co-champion	S. side Mackay Science	40	64	30	119
Northern Red Oak *Quercus rubra*	Champion	Lawn area 50 ft. S.E. of Sarah Fleischmann Building	123	89	88	234
Paperbark Birch *Betula papyrifera*	Up-and-coming	S. side Laxalt Mineral Engineering	18	31	18	33
Red Horse-chestnut *Aesculus carnea* 'Briotti'	Champion	N. and W. of sidewalks in Engineering Quad	63	36	36	108
Vanderwolf Pine *Pinus flexilis* 'Vanderwolf'	Co-champion	N.E. corner Ag Quad	40	44	19	80

SOUTHWESTERN CAMPUS

Common name / Scientific name	Status	Location				
American Hornbeam *Carpinus caroliniana*	Up-and-coming	S. end alcove E. side of Manzanita Hall	15	27	19	47
Crabapple *Malus sp.*	Champion	50 ft. N. of Juniper Dorm & N. Virginia St.	98	25	34	135
Cutleaf Weeping Birch *Betula pendula* 'Laciniata'	Co-champion	Center St. entrance just S. of information booth	83	49	43	143
European (Black) Alder *Alnus glutinosa*	Champion	W. side Ross Hall	56	56	23	118
European Spindle Tree *Euonymus europaeus*	Champion	100 ft. E. and 50 ft. N. of N.E. corner 9th St. and N. Virginia St.	42	25	27	74
European White Elm *Ulmus laevis*	Champion	4th tree W. of Center St. entrance along 9th St.	111	68	39	189

Common Name / Scientific Name	Type of Champion	Location	CBH (inches)	Height (inches)	Spread (inches)	Points
Green Ash *Fraxinus pennsylvanica*	Champion	100 ft. N. and E. of 9th St. & Center St. entrance	118	108	69	243
Kobus Magnolia *Magnolia kobus*	Up-and-coming	30 f. N. of American Hornbeam	14	25	16	43
Ohio Buckeye Horse-chestnut *Aesculus glabra*	Champion	W. side Morrill Hall	52	67	29	126
Purpleblow Maple *Acer truncatum*	Champion	W. side Ross Hall near doorway	69	53	42	142
Scotch Elm *Ulmus glabra*	Champion	Near flagpole 50 ft. S. of Morrill Hall	164	101	82	285
Siberian Elm *Ulmus pumila*	Champion	50 ft. N. and 100 ft. E. of 9th St. and Center St. entrance	155	110	64	281
Autumn Purple Ash *Fraxinus americana* 'Autumn Purple'	Up-and-coming	S.E. corner Clark Administration Building	51	43	45	110
White Spruce *Picea glauca*	Champion	2nd tree from 9th St. along Center St. entrance	83	74	33	165
CENTRAL AND NORTH CAMPUS						
Blue Atlas Cedar *Cedrus atlantica* 'Glauca'	Champion	E. side Mack Soc. Sci., middle of building	94	88	51	195
Dutch Elm *Ulmus x hollandica*	Champion	50 ft. N.W. of S.W. corner Mackay Mines Building	118	88	59	221

Name	Designation	Location				
European Ash Fraxinus excelsior	Champion	50 ft. N. of water feature, Cherry Blossom Garden	80	62	43	153
Japanese Flowering Cherry Prunus serrulata	Champion	S.W. corner Physics Building	43	43	31	91
Smoketree Cotinus coggygria	Champion	Eastern atrium of Medical School	23	39	22	67
Red Jade Weeping Crabapple Malus x scheideckeri 'Red Jade'	Co-champion	50 ft. N. of Ansari Business Building	32	18	22	56
White Alder Alnus rhombifolia	Champion	S. side Ansari Business Building	67	41	37	117
Young's Weeping Birch Betula pendula 'Youngii'	Co-champion	100 ft. N. of Ansari Business Building	27	12	18	44
VALLEY ROAD PARK (EAST SIDE OF VALLEY ROAD, SOUTH OF NEVADA DEPARTMENT OF WILDLIFE)						
Amur Honeysuckle Lonicera maackii	Champion	25 ft. W. of S.E. corner	57	18	26	82
Autumn Olive Elaeagnus umbellata	Champion	30 ft. from S.W. corner	14	16	18	34
Chestnut Oak Quercus prinus	Champion	150 ft. E. and 50 ft. N. of S.W. corner	40	49	96	38
Dwarf Chinkapin Oak Quercus prinoides	Champion	60 ft. W. and 30 ft. N. of S.E corner	28	28	75	84
Sawtooth Oak Quercus acutissima	Champion	150 ft. E. and 100 ft. S. of N.E. corner	40	42	33	90

Totals: 30 Champions, 5 Co-champions, and 7 Up-and-comings

APPENDIX C

Memorial Trees at the University of Nevada, Reno

*Compiled by Tyler Nickl from records archived
in Special Collections, #AC0582, Box 5*

From 1974 to 1991 the Arboretum Board ran a successful Memorial Tree Program, making it possible for a donor to plant a tree in someone's name. This program planted more than 120 memorial trees, representing nearly 100 different species. Below is a list of the honorees, donors, and trees from the Memorial Tree Program, based on archival records. We have chosen to reproduce the archival records for historical interest rather than revising them to reflect current naming practice. Today, the Commemorative Tree Program, established in 2015, once more offers donors the opportunity to honor a special person and support the university's arboretum by planting a tree. (See the arboretum website for details, www.unr.edu/arboretum.)

A University Centennial Commemoration
Donated by the President's Funds through James Anderson
Six Rocky Mountain Bristlecone Pines — *Pinus aristata* / 1974

In memory of **Lt. Col. Roy A. Davis**
Donated by Marjorie L. Davis
European Mountain Ash — *Sorbus aucuparia*
Located at Palmer Engineering Building / 1974

For campus beautification
Donated by Nevada Military Officers' Wives' Club
Red Maple — *Acer rubrum*
Located at Palmer Engineering Building / 1974

In memory of **Lewis and Hazel McCarty LaVoy**
Donated by Mrs. John LaVoy
Scarlet Oak — *Quercus coccinea*
Located at the Rose Garden by the Quad / 1975

In memory of **William T. Sutton**
Donated by his parents,
Mr. and Mrs. William D. Sutton
Pin Oak — *Quercus palustris*
Located at Old Stewart Hall / 1975

In memory of **Edward A. Michal**
Donated by Sylvia McLeod
Austrian Pine — *Pinus nigra*
Located at the southwest corner of
the Church Fine Arts Building / 1975

In memory of **Second Lt. D. Quilici**
Donated by Col. Clifford F. Quilici
and Mrs. June A. Quilici
Crimson King Maple — *Acer platanoides*
Located at Fleischmann / 1975

In memory of **George and May Hennen**
Donated by George Hansen
White Fir — *Abies concolor*
Located at the southeast corner
of the Education Building / 1975

In memory of **Mrs. Johnson's parents**
Donated by Lt. Col. Max K. Johnson
American Chestnut — *Castanea dentata*
Located at the Valley Road site patio / 1975

For campus beautification
Donated by Norma R. Cowlishaw
Gingko — *Gingko biloba*
Located on the east side
of the Education Building / 1975

Donated by Dr. William Van Tassel
Blue Oak — *Quercus douglasii*
Located between MSS and
the Chemistry Building / 1976

Donated by Hal Klieforth
Six Quaking Aspens — *Populus tremuloides*
Located at the Education Building / 1976

For her husband's birthday
Donated by Mrs. Helen Devine
Northern Red Oak — *Quercus rubra*
Located at the northwest corner of
Palmer Engineering Building / 1978

Donated by Robert Slyter
Sixteen Tricolor Beeches — *Fagus sylvatica* 'Tricolor'
Located at the Agriculture Quad / 1976

In memory of **Susan Wood**
Donated by the Psychology Department
Columnar English Oak — *Quercus robur* 'Fastigiata'
Located at the southeast corner of
Mack Social Science Building / 1978

Donated by Dr. and Mrs. Ira LaRivers
Four Rocky Mountain Bristlecone Pines — *Pinus aristata*
Located at the southeast corner of Lombardi / 1978

Donated by Dorothy Benson
Spartan Juniper — *Juniperus* 'Spartan'
Purple Robe Locust
Hawthorn — *Crataegus sp.*
Blireana Plum
All located near the
university's entrance sign / 1978

For **Cecilia St. John,** an advisor for ten years
Donated by the Association of Women Students
Flame Maple — *Acer rubrum*
Located east of Morrill Hall / 1978

In honor of **Dr. Dana,** the C&S Advisor
Donated by S. Gomberg
Beech Tree — *Fagus*
Located at the courtyard
of the Education Building / 1979

In memory of **J. Belle Gorell**
Donated by Mrs. A. Engel
Magnolia Alexandria —
Magnolia soulangeana 'Alexandrina'
Located on the southwest
side of Manzanita Lake / 1979

In memory of **Bruce A. Gould Jr.**
Donated by Mrs. Salley Gould
White Dogwood — *Cornus sp.*
Located at the southeast corner
of Manzanita Hall / 1979

In honor of **Dr. Dano Orvis**
Donated by the Girls Club
Hawthorn
Located at the southwest corner
of the Education Building / 1980

In honor of **Dr. Tom Tucker**
Donated by the university administration
Idaho Locust — *Robinia ambigua idahoensis*
Located on the east side of the Education Building / 1981

In memory of **Jim Haynes**
Donated by Jean Metcalf and Phyllis Hedgepath
Flowering Plum — *Prunus sp.*
Located on the southwest corner
of campus by the university sign / 1982

In memory of **Sigmond Leifson**
Donated by the Physics Department
Colorado Blue Spruce — *Picea pungens*
Located at the west entrance
of the Physics Building / 1984

Donated by Delta Sigma Pi
Blue Atlas Cedar — *Cedrus atlantica* 'Glauca'
Located at the south Manzanita entrance / 1985

In memory of **Bill Phillips**
Donated by UNR Buildings and Grounds
Rocky Mountain Juniper — *Juniperus scopulorum*
On the south side of the Business Building / 1984

In memory of **Helen Perriera**
Donated by Karen Garrell and Sally Carrothers
Mountain Ash — *Sorbus aucuparia* / 1986

In memory of **Lt. Jean Louis Ochoa,** UNPD
Donated by UNR Police Department
Engelman Spruce — *Picea engelmannii*
Located in front of Getchell Library / 1986

In honor of **Mena Porta** for her
dedicated service to students
Donated by Student Services
Tricolor Beech — *Fafus sylvatica* 'Tricolor'
Located in lawn east of Jot Travis Union
behind Thompson Student Services / 1986

Donated by the Board of Regents
Tulip Tree — *Liriodendron tulipifera*
Located at the northeast corner
of the Clark Building / 1986

Dedicated to **Dorothy Benson**
Donated by the Board of Regents
Littleleaf Linden — *Tilia cordata*
Located south of the Getchell Library / 1986

In memory of **William V. Howard**
Donated by Anne, Jason, and Emily Howard
Kousa Dogwood — *Cornus kousa*
Located at the southeast corner
of Mack Social Science Building / 1987

In memory of **Mildred Swift**
The Weeders and Seeders Garden Club
Weeping Goldenchain Tree — *Laburnum* x *watereri vossii*
Located northwest of Home Economics / 1987

In memory of **Lt. Col. William Ryan**
Donated by Grace, Bill, & Virginia Kersey
Higan Cherry — *Prunus subhirtella*
Located on the hillside below pitch flume,
west of A.G. / 1987

In memory of **Ralph Mayo,** father
Donated by Phillip and Rhea Paddelford
Pacific Rainbow Dogwood — *Cornus florida*
Located on the southeast corner
of Mack Social Science Building / 1987

In commemoration of Arbor Day
Donated by the Forestry Club
Rocky Mountain Bristlecone Pines — *Pinus aristata*
Located on the east entrance of the Planetarium / 1987

In commemoration of Arbor Day
Donated by Dr. Ed Kleiner
Raywood Ash — *Fraxinus oxycarpa* 'Raywood' / 1987

In memory of **Clare Parre**
Donated by Thompson Student Services
Taiwan Flowering Cherry — *Prunus campanulata*
Located on the east shore of Manzanita Lake / 1987

In memory of the honorable **Phyllis Kaiser**
Donated by Jan Evans
Sour Gum — *Nyssa sylvatica*
Located on the lawn west of the main
entrance to the medical school / 1987

In memory of parents **Harold "Dutch"
and Margaret "Peggy" Daniel**
Donated by Beverly and Justin Olin
Flowering Plum — *Prunus blireana*
Located near the south entrance
to Manzanita Hall / 1987

In memory of **William Rodgers**
Donated by Ruby Rodgers and
Francis and Patricia Nash
Mimosa — *Albizia julibrissin*
Located between Manzanita
Hall and the lake / 1987

In honor of **Lee Kosso**
Donated by University Special Collections Department
Kobus Magnolia
Located near Getchell Library benches / 1987

Donated by Delta Sigma Pi
Lavender Lilac — *Syringa vulgaris*
Located in the flower bed
south of Manzanita Hall / 1987

In memory of son, **Jamie Domenici**
Donated by the Peter Domenici Family
White Fir — *Abies concolor*
On the east shore of Manzanita Lake / 1987

In connection with an art project
Donated by John Rollof
White Alders — *Alnus rhombifolia*
Located at the north entrance of the Church Fine
Arts Building, inside the fish sculpture / 1987

Donated by Jack Cook, UNR track coach
Columnar English Oak — *Quercus robur* 'Fastigiata'
Located near the west corner of Lombardi Recreation / 1988

In honor of **Anne Amaral**'s service to the university arboretum
Donated by the University Arboretum Board
Copper Leaf Beech — *Fagus sylvatica atropunicea*
Located on the Chemistry Building quad / 1987

In memory of **Judge John E. Gabrielli**
Donated by the Office of Public Information and Publications
Contorted Eastern White Pine — *Pinus strobus* 'Contorta'
Located south of the flagpole in the circle lawn / 1988

In memory of **Eugene S. Faust,** state resident cartographer
Donated by Nevada State Board on Graphic Names
Black Hills Spruce — *Picea glauca* 'Densata'
Located at the bottom of the Ninth Street stairs / 1988

In loving memory of **Jim and Cleo Ronald**
Donated by Ann Ronald
Pyramidal Scotch Pine — *Pinus sylvestris* 'Pyramidalis'
Located at the bottom of the Ninth Street stairs / 1988

In memory of **F. I. Solso**
Donated by the Robert Solso Family
Weeping Crabapple — *Malus sp.*
Located north of the Business Building / 1988

In memory of **Charlie Speth,** father
Donated by the Leland G. Smith Family
Tulip Tree — *Liriodendron tulipifera*
Located on the south end of the Agricultural Quad / 1988

In loving memory of **Col. James P. Pappas, MD, and Anne Pappas**
Donated by the Melick and Kersey families
Eastern White Pine — *Pinus strobus*
East of the entrance to the Family Medicine Building / 1988

In honor of **Judge John E. Gabrielli,**
for dedication to family and community
Donated by the Office of Public Information
Contorted Eastern White Pine — *Pinus strobus* 'Tortuosa' / 1988

In memory of **Millie Qualls**
Donated by Jane Davidson
Weeping Norway Spruce — *Picea abies* 'Pendula'
At the northwest corner of the Church
Fine Arts Building garden area / 1989

In gratitude to the community of
university students, staff, and faculty
Donated by the Dhingra Family
Crimean Linden — *Tilia euchlora*
At the south side of Getchell Library / 1989

For **Steve and Meg Urie**
Donated by Peggy Urie
Redbud — *Cercis canadensis*
Located on the north side of
the Church Fine Arts Building / 1989

In honor of **G. F. "Dick" Coffill**
Donated by John A. and Sheryl Shorter
Rosehill Ash — *Fraxinus americana* 'Rosehill Ash'
Near the computer center / 1989

In loving memory of **William "Doug" Cox**
Donated by John A. and Sheryl Shorter
Moraine Ash — *Fraxinus holotricha* 'Moraine'
At the south end of the Church Fine Arts Building / 1989

In memory of **Courtney D. Joustra**
Donated by her best friend, Courtney Blasey
Japanese Full Moon Maple — *Acer japonicum* 'Aconitifolium'
Located north of Thompson Student Services / 1989

In loving memory of **John William Peterson**
Donated by his family
Amur Maple — *Acer ginalla*
On the southwest shore of Manzanita Lake / 1989

In honor of **Dr. Jack H. Shirley** for thirty years of service to the university
Donated by Admissions and Records staff
Giant Sequoia — *Sequoiadendron giganteum*
On the northeast shore of Manzanita Lake / 1989

In honor of **Frank Meyers, PhD,**
Dean of the College of Education
Donated by Rose Bullis
White Oak — *Quercus alba*
Located south of the Judicial College / 1989

In honor of **Doug Rennie**
Donated by his friends at the Desert Research Institute
Koster Blue Spruce — *Picea pungens* 'Kosteri'
By the stairs at the Scrugham Engineering Building / 1989

In honor of their granddaughter's birthday
Donated by Manuel and Gail Fanjul
White Oak — *Quercus alba*
Located behind the Education Building / 1989

In honor of **Gary and Louise Bullis**
Donated by Rose M. Bullis
Burgundy Liquid Amber
On the north side of the
Church Fine Arts Building / 1989

To **William F. Branstetter**
Donated by Jeff and Chris Courson
Weeping Larch
On the southwest side of the
Sarah Fleishchmann Building / 1989

In memory of **Esther Moyers** for her twenty years
of service to the UNR library, 1959–1979
Donated by Friends of UNR Library
Star Magnolia — *Magnolia stellata*
Located on the south side of Getchell Library / 1989

In honor of **Roberta K. Orkutt**
Library Staff, Faculty, and Friends
Star Magnolia — *Magnolia stellata*
Located on the south side of Getchell Library / 1989

In memory of **Patricia B. Hicks**
Donated by friends and employees at Harrah's
Manregion Walnut — *Juglans regia* 'Manregion'
At the bottom of the Agriculture Building stairs / 1989

In memory of **Willard F. Day,** 1926–1989
Donated by his friends
Purple Leaf Beech — *Fagus sylvatica atropurpurea*
East of Mack Social Science Building in the quad / 1989

In fond remembrance of **Victor and Katherine Vineis**
Donated by the Melick, Kersey, and Ryan families
Spanish Fir — *Abies pinsapo* / 1989

In honor of **Terril J. Kramer, PhD,** in recognition
of his commitment to the arboretum
Donated by the UNR Arboretum Board
Japanese Pagoda Tree — *Sophora japonica*
At the south end of the Mackay Science Building / 1989

In honor of **Roberta Barnes**
Donated by Associated Students of the University of Nevada
Red Twig Dogwood — *Cornus stolonifera*
At the foot of the drive between the
Clark and Frandsen Buildings / 1989

In memory of **Col. Guy F. Cardinelli,** class of 1951
Donated by Patricia Cardinelli
Columnar English Oak — *Quercus robur* 'Fastigiata'
Located on the Agriculture Building Quad / 1989

In memory of **Lillian M. Whalen**
Donated by Jesse Families
Red Japanese Maple — *Acer palmatum* var. *atropurpureum*
On the west side of the Physical Plant / 1989

In memory of **Mercer Ryan**
Donated by his friends in the Reno Flower Arrangers Guild
Silk Tree — *Albizia julibrissin*
On the south side of the Church Fine Arts Building / 1989

In memory of **Patricia E. Chaffin**
Donated by library friends and staff
Northern Red Oak — *Quercus rubra*
On the south side of Getchell Library / 1989

In memory of her beloved mother, **Cornelia Arghir**
Donated by her daughter, Monica Grecu, PhD
Colorado Blue Spruce — *Picea pungens glauca*
On the east side of Manzanita Lake / 1989

In memory of **Bob Sumner**
Donated by Edna and Bruno Benna
Eastern White Pine — *Pinus strobus*
North of the Old Gym / 1989

For **Theresa Celeste Lawson**
Donated by Elizabeth Lawson
Weeping Mulberry — *Morus alba* 'Pendula'
At the south end of Manzanita Hall / 1989

In memory of **Ronald Scott Parker**
Donated by friends at the Sparks Family Hospital
Rocky Mountain Bristlecone Pine — *Pinus aristata*
Located west of the Nevada State Public Health Laboratory / 1989

In memory of **Robert Leland**
Donated by Joy Leland
Pagoda Dogwoods — *Cornus alternifolia*
Southeast of the Clark Administration Building / 1989

In fond memory of **Jeanette Levingston Devine,** 1960–1989
Donated by her coworkers in the College of Business Administration
Columnar English Oak — *Quercus robur* 'Fastigiata'
Near the Laxalt Mineral Engineering Building / 1989

For **Henry G. Frost** for his support of the university
Donated by the Kersey, Colby, Rice, and Galatas families
Common Horsechestnut — *Aesculus hippocastanum*
In the Agriculture Quad / 1989

In memory of **Clara M. Marschall,** beloved wife and mother
Donated by Leonard Marschall
Northern Red Oak — *Quercus rubra*
Located in the Mack Social Science Building Quad / 1989

In memory of **Edith Harris Lovelock**
Donated by the Edith Harris Lovelock Trust
Paul's Scarlet Hawthorn — *Crataegus laevigata* 'Paul's Scarlet'
Located by the Medical School / 1989

In loving memory of **John W. Hudgel**
Donated by Nancy Vannuci
Don Juan Rose — *Rosa* 'Don Juan'
On the east side of the Life Science Building / 1989

In memory of **Thomas Greco**
Donated by the UNR Physical Plant
Douglas Fir — *Pseudotsuga menziesii*
South of the Clark Building, between two spruces / 1989

In loving recognition of **James N. Lowe**
Donated by Lois J. Parker
Japanese Maple
Located by the north entrance of
the Life Sciences Building / 1990

In honor of **Joan Metcalf** on the occasion of her retirement
Donated by the Staff of Student Services
Umbrella Catalpa — *Catalpa burgii*
Near the Planetarium parking lot / 1990

In memory of **Lynette Meyer**
Donated by Friends of Research and Educational Planning
Golden Black Locust — *Robinia pseudoacacia* 'Frisia'
Located west of the Education Building / 1990

In honor of **George Langsner**
Donated by Robert Langsner
Common Hackberry — *Celtis occidentalis*
Next to the phone booth south of the Clark Building / 1990

In memory of **Marion Welliver**
Donated by the Otsuka Family
and Gordon and Anne Stewart
Limber Pine — *Pinus flexilis*
Located near the Planetarium circle / 1990

In memory of **Donald W. Sturdivan**
Donated by Karen Garrell
Contorted Filbert — *Corylus avellana*
In the flower bed left of the
Jot Travis Union entrance / 1990

In memory of **Frank T. Eck Jr.**
Donated by Kate Schulz
Lavalle Hawthorn — *Crataegus lavallei*
Located on the Medical School lawn / 1989

In memory of **Forest and Edith Lovelock**
Donated by the Lovelock Trust
Paul's Scarlet Hawthorn —
Crataegus laevigata 'Paul's Scarlet' / 1990

In memory of **Annebelle Smythe**
Donated by the Crain Family
Bradford Pear — *Pyrus calleryana* 'Bradford'
In the parking circle of the Planetarium / 1990

In recognition of **Andrew Kajans**
Who planted four blue spruces in the 1950s for his grandchildren
Colorado Blue Spruce — *Picea pungens glauca*
Located at the northeast corner of the Manzanita Bowl / Early 1950s

In memory of **Robert M. Moyers**
Donated by his daughter, Sharon Engle
Cutleaf Staghorn Sumac — *Rhus typhinia lanceolate*
South of the Getchell Library / 1990

In memory of **Clifford Shine**
Donated by Linda Ray
Butterfly Japanese Maple — *Acer palmatum* 'Butterfly'
West of the Home Economics Building / 1990

In honor of **Ada F. Taylor,** for her dedicated service to students
Donated by UNR Student Services
Washington Hawthorn — *Crataegus phaenopyrum* 'Cordata' / 1990

In loving memory of **Tiffany Michele Blodgett**
Donated by her mother, Susan Stewart
Japanese Snowbell — *Styrax japonicus*
Located west of the Home Economics Building / 1990

In memory of **Carolyn J. Henderson Martin**
Donated by the Kindred and Dick families
Rosehill Ash — *Fraxinus americana* 'Rosehill'
Near the Benson Gardens / 1990

In memory of **David R. O'Neal**
Donated by Joe and Johanna Crowley
Weeping Mulberry — *Morus alba* 'Chaparral'
Located south of Clark Administration Building / 1990

In memory of **John M. Metcalfe**
Donated by his friends at the University of Nevada Reno
Himalayan Birch — *Betula utilis* var. *jacquemontii*
Located in the Planetarium parking circle / 1990

In memory of **Bob Underwood**
Donated by his coworkers among the Buildings and Grounds staff
Blue Atlas Cedar — *Cedrus atlantica* 'Glauca' / 1991

In recognition of a special award to honor **Virginia Kersey**
Donated with gratitude by the Arboretum Board
European Weeping Beech — *Fagus sylvatica* 'Pendula'
Near the Health Services Building / 1991

In memory of **Anna Walker**
Donated by the Mousel Family
Canada Red Cherry — *Prunus virginiana*
Located in the Planetarium parking circle / 1991

Dedicated to **Robert D. Jeffers** on his
retirement from the university
Donated by Rochelle Horst
Eastern White Pine — *Pinus strobus* / 1991

In recognition of **Bess Beatrice Lowe**
Donated by Dr. Lois Parker
Limber Pine — *Pinus flexilis* 'Vanderwolf'
Located on the northeast corner of
the Agriculture Building Quad / 1991

In recognition of **Zeb Lowe**
Donated by Dr. Lois Parker
Blue Atlas Cedar — *Cedrus atlantica* 'Glauca'
Near the top of the stairs by the Nursing Building / 1991

In memory of **Constance Bernhardt,**
Assistant Director of Career Planning and Placement
Donated by Vada Trimble
Bosnian Redcone Pine — *Pinus heldreichii* var. *leucodermis*
Located at the northeast corner of
Thompson Student Services Building / 1991

In loving memory of **Bruno Hillmeister**
Donated by his friends at the Development Office
Valley Oak — *Quercus lobata* / 1991

For **Andrea and Agnes Hillmeister**
Donated by their friends at the Development Office
Snowdrop Trees — *Halesia carolina*
Located on the east side of Ross Hall / 1991

In memory of **Rose A. Orris**
Donated by Judy and Bill Petterson
White Fir — *Abies concolor* / 1991

In honor of **Samuel Dees Wood,**
for his years of university service
Donated by his friends
Northern Red Oak — *Quercus rubra* / 1991

In loving memory of
Raymond C. Cox, professor emeritus
Donated by the Cox family
Weeping Elm
Located on the Agriculture
Building Quad / 1991

Acknowledgments

JAMES W. HULSE

The tradition of acknowledging individuals upon the completion of a manuscript does not fit here. So many people have participated in the evolution of the university's arboretum that to identify a few would exclude, unfairly, many more. The hundreds who have worked on Buildings and Grounds, the Arboretum Board, the donors and faculty, among others, have been participants—often unknowingly—in this summary of their work. Arbor Day is not limited to the date of its traditional celebration.

CHERYLL GLOTFELTY

A joy of chairing the Arboretum Board and spearheading this book has been working with wonderful people. I cherish them all and regret that space will not permit me to enumerate their individual contributions. A simple roll call of helpers, friends, and family must suffice. For me, each of these names evokes fondness and gratitude. Thank you so much!

Evelyn Acton, Loren Acton, Stan Acton, Kurt Adams, Cami Allen, Lee Bale, Mike Branch, Rozena Brecke, Lynda Buhlig, Bill Carlos, Steve Churchillo, Donnie Curtis, Theresa Danna-Douglas, Jean Dixon, Rebecca Evans, Jinni Fontana, Jodi Fraser, Natalie Fry, Betty Glass, Rosa Glotfelty, Steve Glotfelty, Betty Hulse, Jack Hursh, Wayne Johnson, Davene Kaplan, Ed Kleiner, Robert Landis, Lucas Littlehale, Michael Maher, Raymond Needham, Tyler Nickl, Kelly Norman, Claudia Ortega-Lukas, Dick Post, Justin Race, Eric Rasmussen, Vic Redding, Kirsten Schuhmacher, Marty Sillito, Scott Slovic, Roxie Taft, Curtis Vickers, Christoph Weber, Keiko Weil, Ron Zurek, Matt Zytkoskee, and members of the Arboretum Board.

Extra-special, heartfelt thanks to Jim Hulse and Rod Haulenbeek, who coauthored this book *pro bono* and agreed to donate author royalties to the arboretum.

ROD HAULENBEEK

The author would like to acknowledge some of the many people and entities whose information was essential to this compilation. First, some of the many books consulted include Michael Dirr, *Manual of Woody Landscape Plants*, David More and John White, *The Illustrated Encyclopedia of Trees*, David Allen Sibley, *The Sibley Guide to Trees*, John Stein and Denise Binton, *Field Guide to Native Oak Species of Eastern North America*, and Russell Peterson, *The Pine Tree Book*.

One of the advantages of the Internet Age is the fount of information available. Websites consulted for this book include the Missouri Botanical Garden Plant Finder, Wikipedia, the Gymnosperm Database, Oregon State University, Department of Horticulture, Landscape Plants, Dendrology at Virginia Tech, and J. F. Schmidt Co., as well as a multitude of websites that provided tree images.

Corporate memory was also essential. The University of Nevada, Reno has many resources available, including Ed Kleiner, Dick Post, Davene Kaplan, Tom Stille, and the UNR Special Collections Department.

Lastly, this book would never have been possible without the help of Cheryll Glotfelty, university Arboretum Board chair. She not only had the original idea for the Tree Tours, but she also beta tested each one at least once. The editor of this book, she also has been a constant source of support throughout the book-writing process.

About the Authors

JAMES W. HULSE first visited the University of Nevada, Reno seventy years ago, in 1947, as a high school student attending Boys' State. He was an undergraduate at Nevada from 1948 until 1952. He returned as a graduate student from 1954 until 1958 and as a member of the history department faculty from 1962 until 1997. Twice previously, Hulse has been encouraged to write about his alma mater. In the early 1970s, President Charles J. Armstrong proposed a centenary review of the institution, which sowed the seed for *A Centennial History of the University of Nevada* (1974). A quarter-century later, Chancellor Richard Jarvis planted the idea of an update to mark the 125th anniversary of higher education in the state. From that conversation grew *The System Reinvented: A History of Higher Education in Nevada, 1968–2000* (2002). Only in his emeritus years did Hulse begin to appreciate the rich diversity of the foliage.

CHERYLL GLOTFELTY joined the University of Nevada, Reno English department in 1990 as the nation's first professor of literature and environment. Her scholarly publications, most notably *The Ecocriticism Reader: Landmarks in Literary Ecology* (1996), have helped the field of literary studies engage meaningfully in environmental issues. Her anthology *Literary Nevada: Writings from the Silver State* (2008) showcases Nevada's rich heritage of literature. She has won many teaching awards, including Outstanding Teaching of the Humanities Award, from Nevada Humanities; Nevada Professor of the Year Award, from the CASE-Carnegie Foundation; Nevada Regents' Teaching Award; and the university's

Photo by Christoph Weber

F. Donald Tibbitts Distinguished Teacher Award. Glotfelty became chair of the university's Arboretum Board in 2014 and since then has become obsessed by trees and passionate about the arboretum.

ROD HAULENBEEK, also known as "The Tree Hunter," has been interested in trees since his youth. He pursued a career as a geologist for two major oil companies. About twenty years ago, he changed careers to pursue his interest in trees. He has published three books about trees, is heavily involved in the Nevada Big Tree Program, and has completed tree inventories for the Nevada Division of Forestry of over 15,000 trees with over 200 species. His certifications include Master Gardener, Tree Worker, Arborist, and Tree Risk Assessment. Rod has documented over 190 tree species on the university's campus and created twenty-eight self-guided, audio tree tours, available on the "Rod's Tree Tours" page of the University of Nevada, Reno Arboretum's website.